JEWS IN A
CHANGING
NEIGHBORHOOD

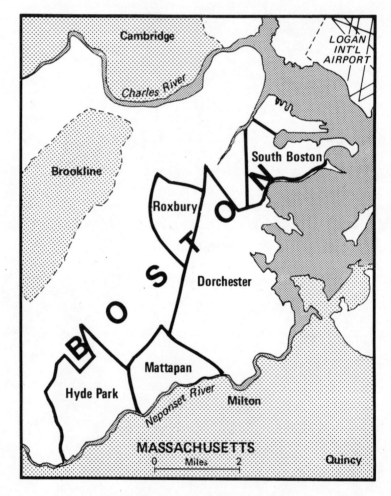

Mattapan and Environs

YONA GINSBERG

JEWS IN A
CHANGING
NEIGHBORHOOD

The Study of Mattapan

THE FREE PRESS
A Division of Macmillan Publishing Co., Inc.
NEW YORK

Collier Macmillan Publishers
LONDON

To the Memory of My Father

The Free Press
A Division of Macmillan Publishing Co., Inc.
866 Third Avenue, New York, N.Y. 10022

Collier-Macmillan Canada Ltd.

Library of Congress Catalog Card Number: 74-24368

Printed in the United States of America

printing number
1 2 3 4 5 6 7 8 9 10

Library of Congress Cataloging in Publication Data

Ginsberg, Yona.
   Jews in a changing neighborhood.

   Bibliography: p.
   Includes index.
   1. Jews in Boston--Social conditions. 2. Negro-
Jewish relations--Boston. 3. Mattapan, Boston.
I. Title.
F73.9.J5G56   301.45'19'24074461   74-24368
ISBN 0-02-911720-8

Contents

Preface

When I began this study of the Jewish people who were the last to remain in Mattapan, a community on the southern border of Boston, Massachusetts, I had only a slight idea of what the study would be like. I wanted to understand what it was like for Jewish people, many of them elderly, to live in a racially changing neighborhood. As it turned out, I was actually dealing with a phenomenon which is not necessarily unique to a changing neighborhood but is part of a much broader urban scene. If one can summarize in four words what life was like for the Jews I interviewed, the best way would be "to live in fear." When I began this research I certainly had no idea how painful the situation would be for these people. I suddenly realized what it means when your whole life is dominated by fear. To be honest, if I had known how stressful and painful the research setting would be, I doubt that I would have begun this study.

Although I may never fully comprehend what it is like to live in fear, I felt that to some extent I was experiencing the same anxieties reported so vividly by the people I interviewed. I tried to see the situation from their point of view and to report their experiences and feelings as honestly as I could. The experience of living in fear, which I have tried to describe in this book, is very easily forgotten. When I read my field notes six months after I had written them, I could hardly believe that I had been so scared. Yet, when I carried out the interviews, the situation was very real and frightening.

This study gives only part of the picture of Mattapan. I dealt only with one group in the neighborhood—with the Jewish people who remained at that time in the area. I did not study the incoming black residents nor the white non-Jewish people. In order to get the whole picture of life in a transitional area, it is essential to do a comparative study of all groups involved in this process. Needless to say, it was impossible for me—a white, Jewish, foreign-born woman—to study any other group under such circumstances. Unfortunately, the efforts of several social scientists in the area to find a black sociologist for this purpose proved unsuccessful. Perhaps this book might stimulate others to carry out similar studies among other groups in changing neighborhoods.

I did the fieldwork in Mattapan between December, 1971, and August, 1972, and wrote it up the following year. The area has not changed much since the summer of 1973. The number of blacks increased somewhat during 1974, and they now constitute the major portion of the population. At the same time, the number of Jews and non-Jewish whites in the area decreased. Since it has become extremely difficult to get mortgages in Mattapan, it seems as if the rapid out-migration has momentarily slowed down. Yet, there are properties for sale on the market, and whites are still trying to move out. Thus, Mattapan is far from being stabilized.

As one drives around the neighborhood it looks as if nothing much has changed. Mattapan Square is still a good shopping area, yet Blue Hill Avenue looks as depressing as it did in 1973. The small residential streets are as clean and nice as ever. The only notable change imposed by the tight mortgage market is that people are unable to get home-improvement loans, and there are some signs of housing abandonment, a very recent phenomenon in Mattapan.

I was very fortunate to be able to do this study while I was a graduate student at Harvard University. Without the help of many people it never could have been done.

I am most grateful to Professor Lee Rainwater for his help, advice, patience, and encouragement. He guided my fieldwork—carried out in a very complicated and sensitive social setting—and helped me find my way through the maze of data.

My special thanks to Professor Lisa Peattie who took an active part in this research from beginning to end. Besides her helpful advice she gave me warm personal support, without which I would not have been able to carry out this study.

Thanks are also due to Professor Nathan Glazer whose advice at various stages of this study proved most helpful, and to Professor Gary Marx for his critical reading of the entire manuscript.

I am particularly indebted to Professor Herbert Gans for his help and advice.

My colleagues at Harvard—Paul Burstein, Diane Barthel, Sherry Rosen, and Judy Lasker—gave me useful comments and editorial help as well as moral support.

The original idea to do a study in Mattapan came from the Joint Center for Urban Studies of MIT and Harvard. I am very grateful to the Joint Center and to its Director, Professor Bernard Frieden, for providing financial support. The completion of the manuscript was made possible by a research grant from the Faculty of Social Sciences of the Tel Aviv University.

Many people in various organizations assisted me in collecting background data on the neighborhood. I received very useful information from the following institutions: the Combined Jewish Philanthropies of Greater Boston, the Equal Opportunities Office of the Federal Housing Authority, the Little City Hall in Mattapan, the Boston Redevelopment Authority, the Mayor's Office of Public Service, the Association for Better Housing, the Mattapan Board of Trade, Boston Police District Three, the Associated Synagogues, and St. Angela's Church. It would be impossible to thank all the individuals who provided me with useful information. My special thanks to Mrs. Patricia Morse of the Equal Opportunities Office of the FHA, to David Farber, Director of the Drop-In Center of the CJP in Mattapan, and to Mrs. Mary Berger, former Director of the Little City Hall.

Charles E. Smith and Eileen Fitzgerald of The Free Press lent professional expertise as project director and production supervisor, respectively, throughout this book's several complex editorial and manufacturing stages.

Finally, I want to thank Mrs. Peggy Polinsky for her careful typing of the final draft of the manuscript and for her editorial help.

Most of all, I want to express my gratitude to the Mattapan Jews, who in spite of fear and suspicion opened their doors to a stranger and let me into their homes. Without their active cooperation, this study could not have been carried out.

CHAPTER ONE

Introduction

Racial transition in residential areas is a widespread phenomenon in American cities. The general pattern of this process is that when black people enter an all-white neighborhood, whites start to move out.

This issue of changing neighborhoods has drawn a wide range of attention from various social scientists, urban planners, policy makers, and from the popular press. Several important questions have been raised regarding this process of racial residential change. The most obvious ones are why does this happen, why do certain neighborhoods change from white to black? Related to this is the question of why white people move out of mixed areas; what are the motives and reasons for their withdrawal?

For someone who is interested in the urban way of life, this phenomenon of residential transition might raise an additional and somewhat different set of questions. It is possible to look at a changing neighborhood from a rather different perspective and ask—what is it like to live in a transitional community? In other words, instead of studying the motives and reasons for the whites' withdrawal, one could focus on those people who have remained in such an area.

Neighborhoods do not change overnight, and although in some cases the change occurs very rapidly, the process of racial residential transition usually continues over some period of time. During this time whites move out and blacks move in. For those whites still living in such areas this means constantly adjusting to the process of change. Little is known about what it is like for those left behind to live in an unstable community. When a changing neighborhood reaches a certain point in the process of racial transition, when the "tipping point" is already crossed, it seems interesting to inquire not only why some white people leave, but why other whites stay in such an area.

This book is about those Jewish people who were the last to remain in Mattapan—a changing neighborhood in Boston. The Jewish population in this area decreased rapidly over a period of four years (1968–1972), from 10,000 to less than 2,500.

The study attempts to describe and analyze a changing neighborhood from the point of view of those who remained in the area. It deals with the process of racial residential transition and its consequences. First, we will describe the process of change from the point of view of the people who experienced it. We will try to understand how they perceive the change and interpret it. Some of the interesting questions asked here are how did the Mattapan Jews realize that their neighborhood was changing, what are the indicators of a changing community, and what are the crucial changes from their point of view? Related to this one could raise another, and perhaps even more interesting, area of questioning: to what extent have these changes in the area had an impact on the way of life of the Mattapan Jews and on their daily behavior; how do they adjust to the changing situation, and how do they cope with it? In other words, this book attempts to understand what it is like for the Jewish people in Mattapan to live in an unstable community.

From the dynamic aspect of the process of change itself as seen and interpreted by the Jewish residents, we will go further and concentrate on the consequences of these changes. The outcome of racial residential change is, of course, that black people are now living in the area. It has been pointed out that "One locale in which racial integration occurs, at least in some form and at least for some short time, is the changing neighborhood on the ghetto's edge." (Molotch, 1972, p. 4.) Since we are dealing with such a phenomenon, this book focuses on the relations between Jews and blacks. Various studies have dealt with this issue, though most of them did not focus on the two groups living in such close residential proximity.

We will attempt to understand the extremely complicated setting of Jews and blacks living in the same unstable neighborhood and the consequences deriving from this situation. Some of the questions asked here are how do the Mattapan Jews perceive the Mattapan blacks, and what are their attitudes toward them? To what extent is there any contact between the two groups, and what are the relationships between Jews and blacks in the area? Thus, this study attempts to describe and understand how the Jewish people of Mattapan feel about the new black residents. As we will see later, the Mattapan Jews find themselves caught in a very painful situation. They feel they have been left behind in the area, and they are frightened. They are hostile and bitter about this situation. Yet, it would be misleading and oversimplified to explain their feelings of hostility in terms of prejudice toward blacks. The situation is much more complicated than that, as we will see. Furthermore, we will show that the Mattapan Jews' attitudes toward the black people are mixed and very complex; they regard blacks as both good and bad and clearly distinguish between their "nice," "respectable" neighbors and the "cheaper class."

Finally, the study attempts to clarify why the Mattapan Jews are attached to the area, what the neighborhood means to them, their plans for their future, and how they view the future of the neighborhood.

The Invasion-Succession Process

Theories dealing with the growth of cities regard interurban migration as a basic component of this process. Burgess' concentric model as well as the sectorial model assume that cities expand outward, from the center to the periphery. According to these theories there are gradients in residential land use from the center outward; the farther away the residential area lies from the center, the better the quality of housing and the higher the socioeconomic status of the residents.

Burgess' model assumes that cities grow mainly through in-migration from outside, especially the in-migration of low-income groups. These groups tend to concentrate first in the zone of transition, "the port of first entry."

> Each new group as it enters the city finds a place of most favorable entry. For all new groups of one or more of the following characteristics—an alien culture, a low economic status and a different race—this point of arrival naturally tends to be in or near the central business district. A commercial district, a business street or a rooming house area puts up notoriously slight resistance to the intrusion of a new group. (Burgess, 1928, p. 109.)

In this zone Burgess notices that the recent immigrant colonies—the "ghettos"—are concentrated. On the first stage of arrival the immigrant groups tend to stick together, segregated from one another and from the rest of the city, whereas later they move outward and are replaced by newcomers.

The spatial movement of various immigrant groups in the

city has been documented in several studies carried out in Chicago in the 1920's and 1930's. Thus, Wirth, studying the Jewish ghetto, observed that

> the zone of settlement of the Jews corresponds roughly to the various generations of immigrants. Those who came earliest are now farthest removed from the original ghetto. They are also furthest away in the process of assimilation and departure of the Old World customs and orthodox rituals. (Wirth, 1928, p. 256.)

Since the zone of transition became the first place of residence for immigrants, its population changed according to the arrival of different ethnic groups. "Group has succeeded group. . . . The Irish Kilgubbern has become the Swedish Smoky Hollow, the Swedish Smoky Hollow a Little Sicily, and now Little Sicily becomes a Negro quarter." (Zorbaugh, 1929, p. 235.)

Burgess regarded the mechanism of this process of change as *invasion* and *succession*. "These population movements from the center to the periphery take the form therefore of successive waves of invasion." (Burgess, 1928, p. 112.) According to this model, the invasion of the new group is met with resistance by the older inhabitants. Although Burgess acknowledged that the more established groups seek better residential areas in the outward zones of the city, he emphasized the "push" factor rather than the "pull" factor. According to his model the expansion of the central business district together with the new waves of immigrants are the major forces which "push" the older immigrant groups from the zone of transition to the more peripheral zones.

Homer Hoyt emphasized more the "pull" factor in the process of urban growth. He observed that "there is a constant outward movement of neighborhoods because as neighborhoods become older they tend to be less desirable." (Hoyt, 1939, p. 121.) The reason that neighborhoods become less desirable with time is that houses deteriorate and become obsolete on the one hand, and new, fashionable neighborhoods are built on the other. The process of neighborhood change described by Hoyt was known later as the filtering or trickle down process. (Aaron, 1972; Lansing, *et al.*, 1969.) The higher income groups move to new and better housing conditions, and their former houses are occupied by lower income groups. In this way, houses filter down the social scale and individuals filter up on the housing scale. It has been demonstrated that in general poor people benefit from the fact that those of higher socioeconomic status have moved into new homes. (Lansing *et al.*, 1969.)

The socioeconomic factor, that is, the desire to improve one's social position by moving into a "better" neighborhood, is not the only reason people move, and as a result, neighborhoods change. Another, not less important, cause for residential mobility is the change in family composition and thus in housing needs. Rossi, in his study in Philadelphia, concluded that "The findings of this study indicate the major factor of mobility to be the process by which families adjust their housing to the housing needs that are generated by the shifts in family composition that accompany life cycle stages." (Rossi, 1955, p. 9.) The study of successive residential moves also indicated the impact of life cycle stages on the choice of housing. Among those who moved to new homes, young couples and elderly people tended to move to apartment buildings, whereas couples with young children preferred a single-family house. (Lansing *et al.*, 1969.)

Racial Succession of Neighborhoods

With the decline of immigration and the increase of the number of blacks moving into cities, the focus of attention of studies on residential patterns has shifted to a large extent from ethnic to racial succession.

Burgess argued that the pattern of residential succession of blacks was basically similar to that of other ethnic groups in the cities:

> The residential separation of whites and Negroes has almost invariably been treated by itself as if it were a unique phenomenon of life. In fact, however, as recent studies clearly prove, this is only one case among many of the working of the process of segregation in the sorting and shifting of the different elements of population in the growth of the city. . . . The city upon analysis is divided and subdivided into residential areas and neighborhoods, each of which is or tends to be predominantly inhabited by some one racial and immigrant group, or economic and social class. (Burgess, 1928, p. 105.)

Nevertheless, studies dealing with residential patterns of different groups in cities clearly indicate that Burgess' conclusion was inaccurate. A comparative study in ten cities demonstrated that the segregation of white ethnic groups from one another as well as from the native white population decreased over time. Blacks were more segregated from native whites and from white immigrant groups than any other ethnic group. The study concluded that "the Negro and immigrant groups have moved in opposite directions, i.e., declining segregation for immigrants and increasing segregation for Negroes." (Lieberson, 1963, p. 132.)

Other studies dealing with residential patterns of different groups confirmed these findings. Taueber and Taueber in their analysis of the ecological dispersion of blacks found a high degree of residential segregation between whites and blacks in Northern and Southern cities in the United States. Their conclusion was that "Negroes are by far the most residentially segregated large minority group in recent American history." (Taueber and Taueber, 1965, p. 68.) In analyzing the pattern of racial segregation over time in different cities, they pointed out that residential segregation increased in the 1940's and decreased only slightly in the 1950's. No substantial differences were found in this respect between Northern and Southern cities.

Residential segregation of blacks could not be explained in

economic terms only. It is evident that they are far more segregated than one could assume on the basis of their economic position. The study of successive residential moves confirmed this assumption. Blacks did not benefit from the filtering process referred to earlier, as whites did. (Lansing *et al.*, 1969.)

Studies dealing with residential patterns in cities share the opinion that the reason blacks are more segregated than any other group is due to the fact that they are excluded from many residential areas and do not have the same choice of housing as whites do. Taueber and Taueber define this situation as a "dual housing market," and use this term in order to explain the relation between race, residential segregation, and income:

> It can be assumed that the supply of housing for non-whites is restricted in terms of both number of units and quality of units. For non-whites, the demand is high relative to supply, and this status is aggravated by the rapidly increasing Negro population. Housing within Negro areas can command higher prices than comparable housing in white residential areas. Furthermore, there has been a continued need for Negro housing, which has been met by transferring property at the periphery of the Negro area from the white housing market to the Negro housing market. The high demand among Negroes for housing combined with the relatively low demand among whites for housing in many of these peripheral areas, makes the transfer of housing from whites to Negroes profitable. (Taueber and Taueber, 1965, p. 25.)

According to this theory blacks pay higher rents for housing in these areas, and this has been demonstrated in various studies. Molotch in his study of the South Shore of Chicago found that black owners paid more for the same houses than whites did, and since the housing choice of blacks is limited, they had to pay a "color tax." He concluded that "the key economic factor of a transition neighborhood is that housing on the market is worth more for blacks than for whites." (Molotch, 1972, p. 20.) Rapkin and Grigsby also found that blacks were usually paying more for housing than whites. (Rapkin and Grigsby, 1960.)

The process of racial residential change of neighborhoods has been analyzed by Duncan and Duncan in Chicago and by Taueber and Taueber in ten cities. Although the Duncans analyze statistical data of the 1940's and the Tauebers of the 1950's, some general conclusions emerge. Both studies demonstrated that the process of racial succession expands in the way that Burgess predicted, that is, from the center to the periphery. Also, the areas entered by blacks are those closest to existing black areas. In both studies it seems that in general the process of racial transition is irreversible; once blacks start moving to certain neighborhoods, those neighborhoods tend to change from white to black. The Duncans observed in Chicago that "areas inhabited by a substantial proportion of Negroes tended to increase their Negro proportion, whether rapidly or slowly, whereas a decrease seldom occurred once an area had reached a proportion of, say, ten percent Negro." (Duncan and Duncan, 1957, p. 11.)

The Tauebers reached the same conclusion: "If racial succession were inevitable and irreversible, Stable Integrated Areas could appear infrequently, and, in fact, such Areas are uncommon in the ten cities." (Taueber and Taueber, 1965, p. 106.) What happens, then, is that over time whites are displaced by blacks, although a pure displacement rarely occurs.

Yet, the process of racial change does not occur overnight. The Duncans distinguish between four stages in the process of racial residential change:

> Referring to the replacement of white by Negro population in a specific area, succession begins with *penetration* by Negroes of an area hitherto inhabited exclusively by whites. When the number and proportion of Negroes become significantly great, *invasion* has occurred. Further increase of Negro population, accompanied by the decrease in the white population amounts to a *consolidation* of the area for Negro residence. Consolidation is completed when the area has become exclusively Negro, or virtually so. A final stage, *piling up*, is recognized if, after complete occupation of an area by Negroes, the Negro population continues to increase, entailing an increase in gross and net population density. (Duncan and Duncan, 1957, p. 11.)

Both the Duncans in Chicago and the Tauebers in the ten cities pointed out that invasion was a highly selective process regarding the socioeconomic characteristics of the black invaders. The Duncans found that blacks with comparatively high socioeconomic status among the invading population moved disproportionally into areas of relatively high status. Therefore, they concluded that "In a sense of a relative comparison among areas, there is a strong resemblance between the characteristics of the invading population and those of the population displaced." (Duncan and Duncan, 1957, p. 15.)

The Tauebers argued that the first blacks that move into an all-white area are of higher socioeconomic status compared to the total black population. Comparing the black population in invasion tracts to that of the whole city, they found that the former was of higher educational and occupational status, tended to own a house, and was less likely to live in crowded housing conditions. They also compared the incoming blacks with the white population in these areas and found that blacks were often of higher educational status than the whites and tended more to be home owners. "Owner occupancy is apparently a major avenue of entering into a new neighborhood." (Taueber and Taueber, 1965, p. 164.)

The selective nature of black entrance was also demonstrated in regard to family composition. A study of the characteristics of blacks in invasion tracts in Chicago between 1950 and 1960 found a relatively high proportion of younger families with children in these areas and concluded that "It appears that younger families lead the way in black residential invasion." (Edwards, 1972, p. 735.)

In spite of the fact that blacks had limited choice in housing and entered usually those white areas peripheral to existing black neighborhoods, it seems that they tended to chose the best areas available to them. Analyzing the characteristics of mixed areas the Tauebers found that "Negro invasion, then, was not limited to deteriorated areas, but occurred in some of the better white areas. However, levels of owner occupancy were lower, and levels of room crowding were higher among whites in invasion tracts than in the rest of the city." (Taueber and Taueber, 1965, p. 157.)

Although both the Duncans and the Tauebers emphasized the relatively high status of blacks leading the way into white neighborhoods, they seem to differ in regard to the characteristics of blacks entering established black areas. In Chicago during the 1940's, black migrants tended to concentrate in "piling up" and in "late consolidation" tracts, that is, in areas with substantial numbers of blacks. These areas, according to the Duncans, were the "port of entry" for the migrant population. Changes occurring in the "piling up" tracts between 1940 and 1950 indicated that the gross population density and the proportion of overcrowded households increased. It seemed that since blacks were confined in several areas and the black population in Chicago increased at that time, the migrants tended to concentrate in areas where a large black population already existed. (Duncan and Duncan, 1957.) According to the Tauebers, this situation changed in the 1950's because of the expansion of the housing market for blacks. The result was that in-migrants did not necessarily concentrate in existing black neighborhoods, and, therefore, the density and crowding in these areas did not increase. (Taueber and Taueber, 1965.)

The Dynamics of Changing Neighborhoods—The Structural Factors

As we have seen, the expansion of the black population in the cities on the one hand and the restrictions on their housing choices on the other are the main causes for the existing racial residential pattern of cities. These factors are external to the neighborhoods themselves. The process of neighborhood change is caused to a large extent by the movement of blacks from existing black neighborhoods to adjacent white areas. Therefore, in accordance with Burgess' model, those areas closest to existing black neighborhoods will be the first to undergo racial change.

Yet, the process of residential racial change does not depend only on the demand for housing by the black population but not less on the housing supply in these areas. The supply and demand of housing for whites has a strong impact on the supply of housing for blacks and thus on the racial residential pattern. The Tauebers observed that

> . . . the greater the rate of Negro population growth relative to white population growth in a city, the more likely an increase in proportion of Negroes in neighborhoods, and the faster the rate of racial change. A high growth rate of white population, relative to Negro population, on the other hand, is accompanied by decline in proportion of Negroes in changing neighborhoods, and a slow rate of racial change. (Taueber and Taueber, 1965, p. 4.)

The rate of residential racial change varies from city to city and from period to period. Thus, as we have seen, the pattern of neighborhood change was different in Chicago in the 1950's than a decade earlier. At that time migration slowed down and the housing market for blacks was less tight. With rapid construction and the white exodus to the suburbs, the demand of whites for housing in the city decreased, and as a result many neighborhoods in Northern cities became open to blacks. This resulted in improved housing conditions for the black population and also in a higher degree of residential differentiation among the black community itself.

Most studies dealing with changing neighborhoods stress the importance of structural variables, mainly those connected with the housing market, as the crucial factors in the process of racial residential change. Those factors account not only for variations in the sociological patterns between cities and in different periods but also for differences in the rate of change of neighborhoods in the same city. The housing market was the main factor explaining variations of racial change in four neighborhoods in Philadelphia. Rapkin and Grigsby found that

Rapid transit in the study areas was the product of numerous influences: liberal mortgage terms, sustained Negro demand, a substantial supply of old houses of fair quality and moderate value, rising prices, considerable activity by professional real estate operators, and ready availability of high quality housing for whites in other sections of the city and suburbs. . . . By comparison slow transition of other neighborhoods was associated with a moderately large percentage of low quality housing for which financing was difficult to obtain, or of expensive houses which most Negro families could not afford. (Rapkin and Grigsby, 1960, p. 117.)

The relatively high prices of the houses was one of the reasons why West Mount Airy, an upper income area in Philadelphia, changed very slowly. Yet this was the only upper income area in the city into which blacks could move because for several years the larger and older houses were for sale at a higher price than the market could absorb. As Rapkin and Grigsby indicated, the incoming blacks were ready to pay the higher prices.

Other studies also indicated the importance of market conditions in the process of neighborhood change. The slow rate of transition in the Bagely Area compared to Russel Woods—both middle-class neighborhoods in Detroit—was in part attributed to housing market and economic conditions unfavorable to residential mobility. (Wolf and Lebeaux, 1969.)

Although, as the Tauebers and Duncans demonstrated, the changing areas were not necessarily characterized by obsolete dwelling units, and middle-class blacks sought the best housing they could get, the segregated housing market imposes some restriction on the quality of housing available. Since blacks mainly move into former dwellings of whites who have moved to newer areas, these dwellings usually tend to be located in the older sections of the city. Despite the fact that some case studies were carried out in middle-class, single-family neighborhoods, these were older and not very fashionable areas. These studies indicated that the neighborhoods started loosing their status even before the blacks moved in, since new suburban neighborhoods

became prestigious. (Mayer, 1960.) In other words, these neighborhoods were no longer attractive to many whites. The South
Shore study in Chicago indicates that despite many efforts to
attract whites to the area, it was impossible to do so. (Molotch,
1972.)

A changing neighborhood is an area in which housing is
being transferred from the white to the black market. It was
assumed that the change of the housing market from white to
black was associated with the decline of property value. Many
studies have dealt with this question. It seems hard to draw
conclusions from these studies because the circumstances of
black entry were not uniform, and the changes of price might be
due to many factors other than race. (Millen, 1973.) Yet, most
studies seem to agree that property value did not decline in
changing neighborhoods. Rapkin and Grigsby found that prices
declined at the first stage of neighborhood change but recovered
later. They concluded that "price decline evidently began in the
white section prior to any reasonable expectations of nonwhite
occupancy in the area. It would seem that most of the downward
shift in prices in these zones was due to factors other than the
threat of Negro entry." (Rapkin and Grigsby, 1960, pp. 100–101.)
Laurenti found that the price changes in mixed neighborhoods
were not uniform and depended on the special circumstances.
Nevertheless, he concluded that "the odds are about four to one
that housing prices in a neighborhood entered by non-whites will
keep up or exceed prices in a comparable all white area." (Laurenti, 1960, p. 52.)

The Behavior of Whites in Changing Neighborhoods

The main theme of many studies of changing neighborhoods
has been focused around the behavior of whites in mixed areas.
One of the questions asked has been to what extent can the
behavior of whites in these areas be explained in the context of

"normal" residential mobility? In other words, to what extent do racial factors account for the behavior of whites in these situations?

Molotch in his South Shore study in Chicago argued that since every American changes his residence each five years, the rate of change in the area had not been affected by the incoming blacks. He compared the mobility rate as measured by property transfer in the South Shore with that of another similar middle-class neighborhood in Chicago not undergoing racial change and found that the South Shore was not less stable than the other area. He concluded that "It is likely that a similar number of persons would have moved no matter what racial conditions existed in the areas." (Molotch, 1969a, p. 236.) The same trend was found in several neighborhoods in Cleveland. (Guest and Zuiches, 1971.) From these findings it seems that racial change could occur in a relatively ordered way. These studies attribute the out-migration rates from mixed areas to nonracial factors such as changes in life cycle stage and housing needs. In these cases the terms "retreat" and "succession" would be more appropriate to describe neighborhood change than "invasion" and "succession." (Johnston, 1971.)

Most studies, however, reported a high rate of mobility in changing neighborhoods. The Tauebers in their comparative study found a high rate of out-migration of whites in invasion tracts compared to the rest of the cities. (Taueber and Taueber, 1965.) The same findings were documented in various case studies in Philadelphia, Detroit, and some areas in Cleveland. (Rapkin and Grigsby, 1960; Mayer, 1960; Wolf, 1960; Guest and Zuiches, 1971.)

A commonly held view is that once blacks move into an all white area, whites panic and withdraw. (Fishman, 1961.) Rapkin and Grigsby demonstrated in a very vivid way what could happen in a neighborhood once the first black family bought a house:

> From there events moved on rapidly. The following morning real estate salesmen were out contacting all home owners in the

block, and by mid afternoon a number of the residents had
decided to sell. A real estate broker who had not solicited any
listings in the block was asked by home owners to list their
houses. (Rapkin and Grigsby, 1960, pp. 141–142.)

The role of the real estate brokers in generating the panic could
not be determined, according to the authors. Various studies
attribute part of the blame to brokers (Wolf, 1957), and one study
even claims that they play a major role in the process of racial
change. "Realtors act not only as 'gate keepers' of statusful
neighborhoods, but also as 'gate crashers' of nonstatusful neighborhoods." (Fishman, 1961, p. 50.) Yet, in some cases neighborhoods changed although there were no reported intensified real
estate activities. This seemed to be the case in Russel Woods in
Detroit (Mayer, 1960) and in the South Shore in Chicago (Molotch, 1972).

The fact that a high rate of out-migration of whites does not
necessarily mean panic selling has been demonstrated in the
Russel Woods case. According to this case study, rapid change
can occur without a panic flight of whites. Three years after the
first black moved in, more than 50% of the neighborhood was
black, in spite of the fact that there was no evidence of panic
selling. Nor, in contrast to some other cases (Bressler, 1960), were
the incoming blacks met with resistance or violence. The author
attributes this to the fact that many of the residents were liberal.
Thus he concluded that "only the rapidity of the turnover of
families distinguished it from 'normal' neighborhood change."
(Mayer, 1960, p. 198.)

Some studies claim that active community organization
might slow down the rate of white out-migration and thus the
rapid change. (Fishman, 1961; Rapkin and Grigsby, 1960.) Yet
Molotch (1972) demonstrated that a very active campaign of a
community organization in the South Shore neighborhood,
which started even before blacks moved into the area, could not
slow down the process of racial transition.

Those case studies try to describe and to some extent explain the behavior of whites in a racially changing neighborhood. Although they do not enable us to give clear-cut answers as to why whites leave mixed areas, they point out some important factors connected with this process.

From the studies it seems clear that the process of out-migration of whites is a selective one. (As was true in the case of in-migration of blacks.) The Tauebers (1965) found that whites of relatively high socioeconomic status tend to move out of changing tracts more than others. The same findings had also been reported in some of the case studies. (Fishman, 1961; Wolf, 1960.) It also seems that the first whites to move out of mixed areas are families with children. (Edwards, 1972.) The quality of schools seems to be a major concern of parents in changing neighborhoods. (Fishman, 1961; Mayer, 1960; Molotch, 1972; Wolf and Lebeaux, 1969.) It is not clear, however, whether many families with children moved out of these neighborhoods before the process of racial change had started. In some neighborhoods at least that seemed to be the case. Molotch (1972) claimed that one of the characteristics of a changing neighborhood is an old-age structure. In these cases white out-migration was due to demographic and not to racial factors.

Differences in the age structure and family composition seem to be one factor explaining different rates of out-migration of whites in changing neighborhoods. The mobility rate of whites was much higher in Russel Woods than in the Bagely Area in Detroit partly because in the latter there was a higher percentage of elderly people who were less inclined to be mobile.

Many studies emphasize the role of predictions and expectations in the moving behavior, or at least in the intentions of whites to move. In Russel Woods, for example, "The selling of the third house [to blacks] convinced everyone that the neighborhood is designated to become mixed." (Mayer, 1960, p. 204.) In a way the very fact that the blacks started moving into the area convinced people that it was not as good as it used to be. Also, the fact that it was close to the black area, and that an adjacent middle-class neighborhood began changing rapidly, confirmed people's suspicions of the future of Russel Woods. This was true to some extent also in the Bagely Area where at the time when the blacks constituted only 10% of the population, "Many people believed that the area was going to be predominantly Negro, and this aspect was one of prime concern to them." (Wolf and Lebeaux, 1969, p. 24.) The authors emphasize that these concerns had nothing to do with the situation at that time in the area. Most people liked the area and were satisfied with their black neighbors. Yet, people were uncertain about the kind of blacks who would move into the area, and their suspicions were reinforced because some of them had previously lived in a changing neighborhood. These expectations seemed to be anchored, at least to some extent, in reality. Wolf and Lebeaux reported that in the case of Lafayette Park, a high-income project close to the black area, whites did not intend to move out despite the fact that it was mixed. The reason was that they expected that only a few middle-class blacks would be able to afford to move into the neighborhood. Thus, they concluded that a "substantial proportion of Negro residents are accepted if they are of similar socioeconomic status and if white residents see little likelihood of the neighborhood becoming predominantly black in the future." (Wolf and Lebeaux, 1969, p. 522.) To some extent this was also true in the case of the Mount Airy Area, an upper income neighborhood in Philadelphia. (Rapkin and Grigsby, 1960.)

In these cases, when people expect their neighborhood to become black, the definition of the situation, that is, that the area is designated to change, becomes very often a "self-fulfilling prophecy." (Wolf, 1957.) The more white people who decide to move out, the more blacks move in, and the more rapid the change.

According to the studies there are several reasons why whites move out of mixed areas, reasons which are connected with the racial factor. The problem of expectations seems to be connected with the fear of whites in remaining a white minority among blacks. Molotch (1972) noticed that if there was resistance to invasion of blacks, it was not to blacks per se, but to complete replacement. Connected with this factor is also the fear of living among people with different values. (Mayer, 1960.) Some case studies of changing neighborhoods which were predominantly Jewish noticed that the desire to live among one's ethnic group seemed to be important for Jewish people. (Mayer, 1960; Wolf and Lebeaux, 1969.)

Some other reasons explaining why whites are reluctant to stay in mixed areas have been reported in the various studies. Some mention the concern of whites regarding property loss. (Fishman, 1961.) Although, as we have seen, property value usually does not drop in a mixed area, the fact that many whites put their property up for sale might result in a surplus supply and therefore in the decline of property values. (Taueber and Taueber, 1965.) The feeling of physical danger and of the decline of safety might be another incentive for whites to move out. (Fishman, 1961; Wolf and Lebeaux, 1969.) Fishman (1961) noticed that sometimes "social factors" such as the fear of status loss and social pressure from the outside contribute to the decision to leave.

The transition of a neighborhood from white to black depends not only on the out-migration of whites and on the in-migration of blacks but to some extent also on the in-migration of whites. In contrast to the general view that whites do not buy in a mixed area, Rapkin and Grigsby found that some whites still bought property in some changing areas in Philadelphia. According to their findings:

> It is not unfair to conclude that families were attracted to the area for commonplace reasons. First and foremost, the families sought a house in a lower price and quality level, and although such dwellings were available in other sections of the city, the choice was somewhat limited. This selection, however, was not made on the basis of the house price alone, but was influenced also by specific advantages of the area such as nearness or ready

access to place of employment, good transportation services, and proximity to a variety of shopping facilities. In addition, many of the purchases were attracted by existing concentration of persons of similar religious or national heritage. In view of these positive factors the white buyers evidently felt the pressure of Negroes was an insufficient reason to avoid the area. (Rapkin and Grigsby, 1960, p. 116.)

It seems that nonracial factors play an important role not only in the decision of whites to move out of certain areas but also in their decision to move in.

Other studies also indicated that whites continue to move into mixed areas. In contrast to the Philadelphia study, however, these studies found that most of the whites who moved in were renters. They moved to their present place of residence because of special advantages to the area, mainly locational advantages, and planned to stay there only temporarily. (Meadow, 1962; Wolf, 1960; Wolf and Lebeaux, 1969.)

This brings us to the question of whether there is a "tipping point" in a racially changing neighborhood. (Grodzins, 1958.) Is there a point at which whites will start moving out faster and will not move in any more? In the Philadelphia case, despite the fact that whites still bought property, it was found that "White purchases were not sufficient to keep the population of the area from becoming increasingly nonwhite." (Rapkin and Grigsby, 1960, p. 116.) They noticed that the white demand for housing in the area did not stop but fell sharply the more the area became black. Thus, it seems that in Philadelphia the proportion of blacks had an impact on the movements of whites. The closer the blacks, the less likely whites were to buy property. Only a few whites bought a house adjacent to a black family.

Wolf (1963), on the other hand, found no "tipping point" in Russel Woods: the proportion of blacks in the area did go up in a steady fashion over a period of seven years. The same results were reported in a study of a changing school in Baltimore where the authors found that "the tipping point is zero." (Stinchcombe *et al.*, 1969, p. 134.)

The Relation Between Behavior and Attitudes

One question most studies ask is what role does prejudice play in the behavior of whites in racially changing neighborhoods? Most studies seem to agree that there is no relationship between attitudes of whites toward blacks and their overt behavior as measured by moving out or remaining in a mixed area. It was found, for instance, that those who moved out of Russel Woods were not more prejudiced against blacks than those who remained in the area. Thus, people with high prejudice were not more likely to move out than others. What seems even more interesting is that those who moved into the area after it had already started to become black did not differ in their racial attitude from those who left or from those who remained. (Wolf, 1960.)

Similar findings were reported by Rapkin and Grigsby in Philadelphia. Although the majority of white buyers were indifferent or approved of the presence of blacks in their neighborhood, those who bought in a mixed area did not seem to be especially liberal. The study noticed that "a large proportion of white families who purchased houses in mixed areas in 1955 had strong objections to the presence of Negroes in their vicinity." (Rapkin and Grigsby, 1960, p. 47.) Although Pettigrew found that "whites are far more likely to move into an interracial neighborhood if they had experienced integration previously" (Pettigrew, 1973, p. 58), that does not necessarily mean that those who move into such areas have more positive attitudes toward blacks. It seems that many factors, other than prejudice, have an impact on housing choices.

Attitudes do not seem to have an impact on the rate of

transition in racially changing neighborhoods: there were no differences in the attitudes of the residents of Russel Woods and the Bagely Area toward blacks, although the former neighborhood changed much more rapidly. (Wolf and Lebeaux, 1969.)

In the Bridgeview study an opposite relation to what one would expect was found between attitude and behavior. Those who moved out of the area were the least prejudiced (as measured by the F-scale), while the most prejudiced remained. It seems that the former were of higher socioeconomic status and could therefore more easily afford to move out of the area. (Fishman, 1961.)

The fact that there seems to be hardly any relationship between attitudes and behavior in regard to integrated housing was also demonstrated on a nationwide level. In spite of the fact that attitudes toward residential integration (as measured by public opinion polls) has become much more favorable in the last decade, the extent of racial residential segregation has not decreased. (Pettigrew, 1973.) A nationwide survey of integrated neighborhoods concludes that "behavior at least as far as residential choices is concerned, is relatively independent of attitudes." (Bradburn et al., 1971, p. 124.)

Most studies also challenge the hypothesis that residential contact with blacks will improve racial attitudes. The attitudes of whites living for several years in close contact with blacks did not improve over time. Also, the most prejudiced whites seemed to be in some cases those who lived in all black blocks, that is, in very close contact with blacks, while the least prejudiced were those who lived in completely white blocks. (Wolf, 1963; Fishman, 1961.) Similar findings were found in a nationwide study of integrated neighborhoods: the whites living in areas with a substantial number of blacks had a somewhat less favorable attitude toward blacks than those living in areas with only a small number of blacks. (Bradburn et al., 1971.) An exception to this pattern is the study of white buyers in Philadelphia in which it was found that among those who moved to a mixed area, those who bought their house in a mixed zone had a somewhat more positive attitude toward blacks living in their area than those who bought their house in an all-white zone. (Rapkin and Grigsby, 1960.) The difference might be due to the fact that those people bought a house voluntarily in the close vicinity of blacks. It is interesting to mention in this context that the major evidence confirming Allport's "contact hypothesis" (Allport, 1958) (that is, that interracial contact might lead to greater acceptance under certain circumstances) seems to derive from studies carried out in housing projects that had been planned from the beginning as integrated communities. (Deutsch and Collins, 1951; Pettigrew, 1969.) This situation, however, seems to be totally different from that in which blacks enter an already established white neighborhood.

Housing choices seem to be influenced by many factors, of which attitudes and prejudice are only one, and apparently not the most important. From the studies on changing neighborhoods there is only very little evidence that behavior in regard to residential preferences is related to attitudes. It seems that one can adopt the Tauebers' conclusion that "any 'tipping point' would thus seem to have less to do with levels of racial tolerance among whites than with the levels of supply and demand for housing in areas that will accept Negro residents." (Taueber and Taueber, 1965, p. 4.)

From all these studies it seems clear that ecological factors connected with the housing market, as well as demographic factors, contribute more to the process of neighborhood transition than the behavior of the white residents in these areas. Neighborhoods do change, whether the rate of out-migration is a "normal" one or whether there is panic selling connected with mass flight of whites. What seems to be more important in such situations is that this process is irreversible. Although quite a large number of mixed neighborhoods were found in the nationwide survey, most of these areas had less than 10% blacks among their population. However, in most cases, as we have seen, once areas start changing they tend to become more and more black.

Molotch's conclusion regarding the transition process of the South Shore in Chicago seems to fit this process in many other communities:

> Racial change patterns are determined by ecological forces beyond the local community. . . . Normal mobility makes neighborhood racial change possible; when markets are structured in such a manner that blacks continuously constitute the bulk of those who move into the resulting vacancies, racial change is inevitable. (Molotch, 1972, p. 172.)

CHAPTER TWO

The Neighborhood

Mattapan lies on the southern border of Boston, Massachusetts, adjacent to Milton. Its generally recognized boundaries are Morton Street on the north, a line south from the junction of Morton Street and Gallivan Boulevard on the east, the Milton line and Cummings Highway on the south, and Harvard Street on the west. The area lies on both sides of Blue Hill Avenue with a large shopping center on Mattapan Square (see map on p. 26).

For the most part, Mattapan looks like a semisuburban area located inside the city. This is mainly true for the southern part of the neighborhood (census tract 1010) where most of the houses are one- and two-family homes, over half of them built in the 1950's or later. The small streets in this section are clean with a lot of green and open space between the houses. Most houses seem to be in good condition and very well kept. In addition, there are in this section several fairly new apartment buildings of about 450

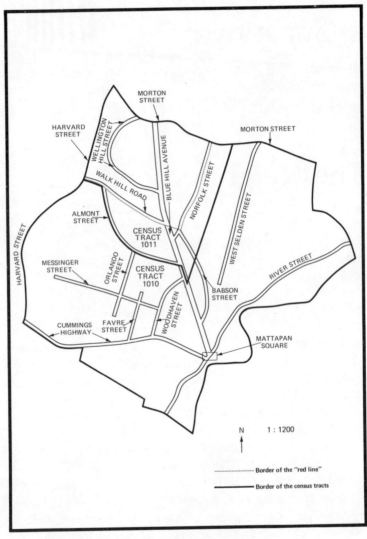

MORTON
STREET

HARVARD
STREET

MORTON STREET

WELLINGTON
HILL STREET

BLUE HILL AVENUE

NORFOLK STREET

WALK HILL ROAD

WEST SELDEN STREET

ALMONT
STREET

CENSUS
TRACT
1011

HARVARD STREET

MESSINGER
STREET

ORLANDO
STREET

CENSUS
TRACT
1010

RIVER STREET

BABSON
STREET

WOODHAVEN
STREET

CUMMINGS
HIGHWAY

FAVRE
STREET

MATTAPAN
SQUARE

N   1 : 1200

.... Border of the "red line"

──── Border of the census tracts

The Mattapan Community

to 500 apartments. A large part of these units is concentrated in two big apartment complexes on the southern edge of the neighborhood. One of these is quite luxurious.

The northern part of the area (census tract 1011) closer to Morton Street is older. Many of the houses are three-decker wooden structures, built mainly between 1910 and 1930. Some of these houses look run down and in poor condition. The buildings were built close to one another with very little open space between them. Some streets in this section look dirty and neglected. Nevertheless, not all streets in the northern section are in poor condition. A few streets in this section are clean, and the houses—although built in the 1930's—seem to be in good condition.

The difference between the two areas of Mattapan is clearly demonstrated when one compares the year the structures were built and the number of units in them, in census tract 1010 and 1011 (see Table 1).

Of the housing units in census tract 1010, 38.2% were built before 1940, compared to 76.2% in census tract 1011. On the other hand, half (50.8%) of the units in census tract 1010 were

TABLE 1
Housing Units by Year Structure Was Built
(in Percentages)

Year	Total	Census Tract 1010	Census Tract 1011
1969–70	0.8	1.2	0.3
1965–68	9.3	14.5	3.0
1960–64	9.6	14.0	4.2
1950–59	13.9	21.2	4.8
1940–49	11.2	11.5	11.4
Before 1939	55.0	38.2	76.2
Number of units	6994	3876	3118

Source: U.S. 1970 Census of Population and Housing.

TABLE 2

Housing Units by Number of Units in Structure
(in Percentages)

Number of Units in Structure	Total	Census Tract 1010	Census Tract 1011
1	18.6	28.2	6.7
2	29.4	36.7	20.3
3–4	28.0	7.9	52.9
5–49	20.5	21.3	19.5
50+	3.5	5.9	0.6
Number of units	6994	3876	3118

Source: U.S. 1970 Census of Population and Housing.

built in the 1950's and 1960's, compared to only 12.3% in census tract 1011. It seems interesting that 15.7% of the housing units in census tract 1010 were built between 1965 and 1970. These are mainly the large apartment buildings on the southern edge of the neighborhood (see Table 2).

Of the housing units in census tract 1010, 64.9% are either single- or two-family houses, compared to 27% in census tract 1011. The typical home in this area is in a three- and four-family apartment building, that is, in a three decker. Although it is not possible from the census data to distinguish between the larger apartment buildings (5 to 49 units), it seems that in census tract 1010 the units in this category are mostly in the new large apartment buildings, whereas in census tract 1011 the units in the category are in the old six-family houses.

The commercial area of Mattapan consists (or rather consisted) of two parts. The strip along Blue Hill Avenue was the main commercial area in the past. It was characterized by small, one-owner stores. The second part of the commercial area centers around Mattapan Square with its bigger stores, such as department stores, and its banks, restaurants, and other services.

The Population

Although the 1970 census is no longer accurate, it is the only reliable source regarding the Mattapan population. The total population of the neighborhood was 20,617 in 1970 (compared to 19,086 in 1960).

Race

According to the 1970 census, 24.8% of the population was black, compared to 0.4% in 1960. Most blacks were at that time concentrated in the northern part of Mattapan (census tract 1011), as the following numbers indicate (see Table 3).

Almost half of the population of the northern part of Mattapan was already black in 1970 as compared to 5.2% in the southern part.

It is impossible to deduce the ethnic composition of the white population from the census. The white population consisted of two main groups: Jews on the one hand, and Irish and Italian Catholics on the other. In 1968 it was estimated that 5% of the population was black, 55% Jewish, and 40% Irish and Italian Catholic.[1] Comparing these estimates with the 1970 census it

TABLE 3
Population by Race
(in Percentages)

Race	Total	Census Tract 1010	Census Tract 1011
White	75.2	94.8	51.8
Black	24.8	5.2	48.2
Total Population	20,617	11,189	9,428

Source: U.S. 1970 Census of Population and Housing.

seems that the black population of Mattapan increased from 5 to 25% in about two years. It is estimated that in 1972 the black population constituted over half of the total population of Mattapan.

Age

The white population of Mattapan seems to be an aging population (see Table 4).

TABLE 4
Median Age of Mattapan Population—1950, 1960, and 1970
(in Years)

	White		Black	
	Male	Female	Male	Female
1950	33.5	35.7	—	—
1960	36.3	37.8	—	—
1970	43.7	45.4	20.6	19.5

Source: U.S. 1950, 1960, and 1970 Census of Population and Housing.

The median age of the white population increased by ten years in the last twenty years. The main change in the age distribution of the population occurred between 1960 and 1970, probably as a result of out-migration of younger people. Mattapan has a very high concentration of elderly white people: 26.8% of the total white population was sixty years or older in 1970. The share of elderly people increased from 16.5% in 1960. The median age of the white population in 1970 was more than twice as high as that of the black population in the area.

Family Size

The fact that the young white families tended to leave meant that those families who remained in the neighborhood tended to be the smaller families. The median size of a white family dropped from 3.2 in 1960 to 2.7 in 1970. The incoming black families on the other hand were larger: their median size was 3.5 in 1970. (It was for this reason that the blacks accounted for 24.8% of the total population but for only 20% of the households.)

The population of Mattapan seems to consist of small, elderly white families on the one hand, and young, quite large, black families on the other.

Socioeconomic Status

The socioeconomic level of the black population of Mattapan in 1970 seemed to be quite similar to that of the white population. The median years of schooling for both groups was 12.1, and the median income level was $9,552 for a white family compared to $8,779 for a black one. Most of the people in the labor force, whites and blacks, seemed to belong either to the working class or to the lower middle class (see Table 5).

TABLE 5
Labor Force by Occupation
(in Percentages)

Occupation	White	Black
Professional	12.1	11.4
Managerial	7.7	4.6
Sales and Clerical	42.1	29.7
Blue Collar	38.1	54.3
Total Labor Force	6936	1990

Source: U.S. 1970 Census of Population and Housing.

Only a small proportion of the working population is in the professional or managerial category; the vast majority are either sales and clerical or blue-collar workers. Blacks tend to have more blue-collar occupations, whereas a higher proportion of whites are clerical or sales workers. (Blue-collar workers, both whites and blacks, consisted mainly of craftsmen, foremen and kindred workers, operators, and service workers.)

The occupational characteristics of the white population of Mattapan has not changed much since 1950. The majority of the working population was then, as now, blue-collar and sales or clerical workers. At least since 1950 Mattapan has been a working-class and lower middle-class neighborhood.

Length of Residence

The majority of the population, 69.3% of the whites and 98.0% of the blacks, moved into its present dwelling units between 1960 and 1970. Only 12.4% of the white population has been living in its present homes since 1950 or earlier.

As one could expect, the majority of blacks (82.2%) moved into its present houses or apartments between 1968 and 1970. Although it is impossible to tell from the census data where the blacks moved from, it is quite certain that they lived previously outside of Mattapan. Interestingly, over a quarter of the whites (28.5%) also moved to their present homes during the same period of time. In contrast to some stable working-class communities, it seems that the Mattapan residents have been quite mobile.

Housing Conditions

As already indicated, in 1970 most of the blacks lived in the northern part of Mattapan (census tract 1011) where the majority of houses were built in the 1930's or earlier. According to the 1970 census, 83.7% of the black households lived in housing units which were built prior to 1950, compared to 61.1% of the white households.[2]

Despite differences in age, all housing units in Mattapan have public water and sewage and plumbing facilities. Eighty-seven percent of the units have central heating. According to the 1960 census, 95.5% of them were in sound condition.

Of the black housing units in Mattapan in 1970, 38.5% were owner occupied compared to 34.7% of the white housing units. In census tract 1011, however, where most blacks lived in 1970, 37.0% of the black housing units were owner occupied compared to only 24.2% of the white units. One could guess from these figures that white owners tended to leave sooner than white renters.

The median size of the dwelling units was 5.6 rooms for the black household compared to 5.0 rooms for the white household. As the black families were usually larger than those of the whites, their housing density was higher. Yet, in only 10.1% of the black households was the density higher than one person per room.

The Jewish Population

The Jewish population of Mattapan was in the past mainly concentrated in the northern part of the area (census tract 1011 and part of census tract 1010). Jews started moving into the northern part of Mattapan after World War I, replacing Yankee families. Later, however, when many new single ranch-style houses were built in Mattapan, the Jewish community expanded toward the southern part of the area. Some Jewish people bought houses in the predominantly non-Jewish section of the area, but they were a minority. When the new apartment buildings were built in the late 1960's, close to Mattapan Square, they were populated to a large extent by Jews. As a result the core of the Jewish population moved southward.

The Jewish neighborhood of Mattapan was in the past a part of the larger Jewish community of Roxbury and Dorchester. This area "centering along Blue Hill Avenue from Grove Hall to Mattapan Square was long the major center of Jewish life. Ten years ago approximately fifty thousand Jews lived in this section, served by almost eighteen congregations, almost all Orthodox."[3] In the 1950's this area was considered the largest Jewish community in New England.

In the 1950's and 1960's, however, Jews began moving out to the suburbs. A 1965 survey of the Jewish population of the Greater Boston Area found that "the Dorchester and Mattapan sections of Boston are no longer the area of greater concentration of Jews. . . . Only 14,000 Jews remain in these areas." (Axelrod *et al.*, 1967, p. 20.) The Jewish exodus resulted in the disappearance of Jewish institutions. In 1967 a newspaper article entitled "Jewish Community Exodus Leaves Temples Deserted," reported that in the previous eight years six synagogues had been disbanded and nine Hebrew Schools had closed since 1950. The article quotes a local rabbi as saying, "For a while as rich Jews moved out, poor Jews moved in, but as the community deteriorated, Jews stopped moving in and just moved out." The reason for Jews not moving into the area was, according to the same source, "the educational level of the schools."[4] The 1965 survey also noted that Jewish people from other places in the Greater Boston Area did not move to this section any more. (Axelrod *et al.*, 1967.)

At that time, however, it seemed that Mattapan proper had not yet been affected by the Jewish exodus to the suburbs. As a matter of fact, Jews tended to move into Mattapan during this period. The Greater Boston Area survey estimated the number of Jews in Mattapan proper in 1965 as 8,500. In 1968, however, it was estimated that about half of the Mattapan population, that is, about 10,000 people, was Jewish.[5] As we have seen, 20% of the housing units were built in the 1960's. Thus, although Jews did not move to the Dorchester-Mattapan area from other places, they still moved to Mattapan proper from Dorchester and Roxbury. As the 1967 newspaper article observed: "All that remains of the flourishing Jewish community is the overflow Morton-Mattapan section. Here too is the Kosher shopping strip owned generally by community shopkeepers."[6] The article goes on to observe that, "The area is currently thriving but its characteristics are changing. Young people are moving out and it is gradually becoming a community of older people."[7]

The size of the Jewish community in Mattapan decreased rapidly after 1968. It is estimated that the number of Jews in the area dropped from about 10,000 in 1968 to less than 2,500 in 1972.

The fact that in 1965 the whole area was already a community of older people was demonstrated by the Greater Boston Area survey. Despite the fact that the survey did not separate Mattapan from Dorchester, its findings seem to be reliable:

> Dorchester-Mattapan is an aging population. About 40 percent of the population is over 50. Young adults are absent, only the teens show a sizable number. The Jewish population in the area is a declining one. Those who are teenagers will leave the neighborhood in a few years and the youngest age group is insufficient to replace them. The population will decline as death takes its toll in the upper age groups. (Axelrod *et al.*, 1967, p. 28.)

As we have seen, 26.5% of the total white population of Mattapan was sixty years old or older, and one could assume that these figures would be even higher for the Jewish population. As a result of the concentration of an elderly Jewish population in Mattapan, only 39% of the households included minor children in 1965. There was also a relatively high concentration of first-generation immigrants in the area—37% of the Dorchester-Mattapan Jewish community compared to 22% of the Jewish population of the Greater Boston Area in general.

Socioeconomic Class

The occupational distribution of the Jewish population in 1965 indicated that the Jewish community of Dorchester-Mattapan consisted mainly of working-class and lower middle-class people. In this respect it seemed that the Jewish population was not different from the general white population in the area. Yet, the occupational distribution of the Dorchester-Mattapan Jews seems to be very different from that of the Jewish community of the Greater Boston Area in general (see Table 6).

Only 11% of the heads of Jewish families in the labor force of

TABLE 6
Occupation of Heads of Greater Boston Area Jewish
Families in the Labor Force (1965)
(in Percentages)

Occupational Category	Dorchester- Mattapan	Greater Boston Area—Total
Professionals	11	31
Managers and Proprietors	26	37
Clerical and Sales	27	20
Blue Collar	34	12

Source: Axelrod, 1967, Tables 4.8 and 4.10, pp. 42–43.

Dorchester and Mattapan were professionals in 1965, compared to 31% of the general Jewish population of the Greater Boston Area. On the other hand, 34% were blue-collar workers compared to only 12% of the total population. The survey concluded that Dorchester-Mattapan is one of the few neighborhoods in Greater Boston where a significant number of Jewish blue-collar workers can be found. The difference in occupation would be even greater if one compared Dorchester-Mattapan with areas such as Newton (a suburb west of Boston with a large Jewish community).

The median income of the Dorchester-Mattapan Jews was $7,620 in 1965, compared to $9,232 for the total Jewish community in 1965.

The fact that more than a third of the Dorchester-Mattapan heads of households were blue-collar workers seems to be significant. In this respect, they seem to differ not only from the Greater Boston Area Jewish community, but also from the Jewish community in the United States in general. Many studies emphasized the relatively high socioeconomic status of the Jews in America. Studies carried out in various Jewish communities around the country during the 1960's indicated that a large proportion of the Jewish population held professional and managerial positions. The percentage of clerical workers seemed to decrease, and only a small proportion of the Jewish labor force was found to be blue-collar workers. (Goldstein, 1971.)

In the 1950's a high proportion of Jews in nonmanual occupations had already been found. Jewish workers, on the other hand, were represented in that period in a sizable number only in the largest cities. Jews achieved their high socioeconomic status in a relatively short period of time. Although Jews arrived in this country later than other immigrants, they were in general more mobile than other ethnic groups. (Glazer, 1960.)

Despite these statistics it is important to note that recently attention has been drawn to the fact that there are still poor Jews in the United States. A survey in New York indicated that "272,000 individuals or 15.1 percent of the Jewish population of 1.8 million in New York City are poor or near poor." (Levine and Hochbaum, 1974, p. 2.) Many of the Jewish poor are elderly.

Changes in the Neighborhood

The impact of the Jewish exodus to the suburbs was not felt in Mattapan proper until the late 1960's. As we have seen, many new apartments were built at that time and Jews continued moving into the area. The black population of the area was estimated as 5% of the total population in 1968. Yet, this proportion increased to 25% in 1970.

Dorchester began changing much earlier. Although no data is available for the late 1960's, according to the census, the percentage of blacks in the two census tracts in West Dorchester on the Mattapan border increased from 9.3% in 1960 to 71.7% in 1970.

This drastic change in the adjacent area had an impact on the residents of Mattapan proper. First, the racial change was accompanied by other phenomena. It was reported that the

> . . . incidents of personal crime—handbag snatching, mugging, vandalism, theft—has increased in the neighborhood, mostly north of Morton Street [the northern border of Matta-

pan]. The Jewish residents have reacted, in part, in panic, because they have been accustomed to an unusually safe neighborhood. The fear of crime far outpaces the actual increase in crime. There is a great deal of racial animosity connected with this fear.[8]

Second, due to open enrollment, about a third of the students at the Lewenberg Junior High School were black in 1966–67, and their number was increasing.

It seems that these factors led to the formation of The Mattapan Organization in the summer of 1967. This was "a neighborhood association dedicated to making Mattapan a high quality, ethnically integrated community."[9] This association was under the sponsorship of the Jewish Community Council of Metropolitan Boston. As we learned later, The Mattapan Organization failed to stabilize and integrate the neighborhood and dissolved at the end of 1969. "Too little too late was the reaction of those who tried to integrate and stabilize the community."[10] Most of the Jewish people who were active in The Mattapan Organization have since left the neighborhood.

During the years in which The Mattapan Organization was active, the neighborhood began changing very rapidly, and over 4,000 blacks moved into the area between 1968 and 1970. From 1969, the press began dealing with Mattapan proper, and articles entitled "Mattapan Problem? Takeover by Blacks"[11] appeared in the newspapers. It was assumed that one of the reasons for this rapid change was the BBURG (Boston Banks Urban Renewal Group) program and the real estate activities in the area. Both were subject to a Senate investigation in 1971.

The Boston Bank Urban Renewal Group (BBURG)

In 1968, after the murder of Martin Luther King, Jr., twenty-two of the Boston banks, responding to the Mayor's appeal, decided on a large-scale mortgage program. As the spokesman of the banks put it in the Senate hearings, "BBURG was born in answer to an appeal by city officials and the community to help rebuild the area of the city that was festering with decay."[12] The bankers mentioned two purposes of the program:

> The goals of BBURG have been and are to save a deteriorating urban area and make a dream of owning a home a reality. BBURG brought home ownership to those who could not afford it. This home ownership breathed new life into the area, preventing it from becoming a municipal burden. In addition the program curtailed absentee ownership and the slum landlord.[13]

The banks decided to allocate $20 million in mortgage money to families who wanted to buy homes. During the years that BBURG operated, the sum was expanded to $29 million. The BBURG loans were insured by the Federal Housing Administration. The mortgages were given under section 221(d)(2) of the National Housing Act of 1934 as amended in 1954. These loans were given with very low down payments: 3% of the first $15,000 of the cost of the house, 10% of the next $10,000, and 20% of the next $10,000. The mortgages were given for twenty to twenty-five years with the usual interest rate. In addition the banks charged a 1% service charge ("point") from the buyer. For many families this meant buying a house with a very low down payment. According to BBURG, about two thousand people were given these FHA mortgages in a period of somewhat over two years.

The mortgages were, however, limited to several areas in Boston: Roxbury, Dorchester, Jamaica Plain (a neighborhood in Boston north of Mattapan), and part of Mattapan. Only people buying inside this "red line" were eligible for the BBURG mortgages. The "red line" later came under attack by public and private sources and was a controversial issue during the Senate hearings. The bankers offered several explanations for the boundaries of the "red line." According to them, the mortgage program originally started in the Washington Park Renewal area and the Model City neighborhoods. This area had been expanded in 1968 to adjacent areas lying south and east of the Model City neighborhoods because there was not enough decent housing in this area.

The bankers explained that as their funds were limited, they had to restrict the mortgages to these areas. Another reason to expand the area beyond Model Cities was, according to them:

> To take in white neighborhoods so that there would be no reference to discrimination against whites, whereby Model Cities and Washington Park were predominantly black neighborhoods. The streets were just arbitrarily picked because they looked long, they looked conspicuous and Walk Hill Street was just to the south.[14]

The bankers, however, admitted that there was a difference in the housing stock—whereas most of the houses inside the "red line" were wooden-frame triple deckers, many houses outside the line were single ranch homes.

The "red line" more or less covered the Jewish neighborhoods of Boston and cut Mattapan in the middle. Besides the whole Jewish area of Dorchester, part of Jewish Mattapan was included, mainly the old three-decker houses. Seven out of eight block-groups of census tract 1011 were included, a total of 2,584 housing units. The bankers claimed that the boundaries had nothing to do with the characteristics of the residents living inside the boundaries. Critics, however, rightly pointed out that "the impact of BBURG did not fall on Brighton-Allston, the North End, or Southie. It fell on predominantly Jewish Mattapan-Dorchester."[15]

One of the bankers' arguments was that "a great portion of the area was black to begin with except for those certain areas near the periphery,"[16] and that it seemed to them only natural to give the mortgages in sections where blacks already had been moving in. As we have seen, the Jewish population of Dorchester and Mattapan declined in the 1960's, and only 14,000 Jews lived in these areas in 1965. As Jewish people moved out, their places were in most cases taken by blacks. In 1967, before the BBURG program, it was noted that "there are approximately 80,000 Negroes in Boston, the vast majority concentrated in Roxbury, North Dorchester, and the South End."[17]

This ecological process of blacks moving into Jewish neighborhoods does not seem to be unique to Boston. Although studies on racial succession do not usually distinguish between white ethnic groups, the fact that blacks moved into a Jewish neighborhood has been pointed out by the popular press.[18]

It is not clear when the "red line" began attracting public attention. A former resident of Mattapan testified that she had heard about the line a year after BBURG started its program.[19] It is also unclear when the existence of the line was brought to the attention of the Jewish organizations of Boston. The "red line" was sharply criticized by white and black residents of the area. Blacks claimed that the BBURG program was operating to restrict black people's choice in housing and to force them to buy in a certain area; that it was discriminatory and that black buyers were being "ghettoized."[20]

Another interesting fact was that although the mortgages were theoretically designated to everybody buying inside the line—the only restriction was the price of the house (no more than $35,000 for a house)—practically all of the mortgages were given to blacks. A home-ownership survey indicated that only 13% of the BBURG buyers were whites.[21] The public view was that the loans were designated for blacks only, and some whites even complained that they could not get an FHA mortgage.[22]

The impact of the "red line" on Mattapan is not clear. It is true, as the bankers noted, that the "natural" migration trend of blacks was toward Mattapan, and that they had already moved to Dorchester before the BBURG program began. The ownership survey of BBURG buyers suggested that "there is no evidence that the buyers 'gave up' the location where they preferred to live in order to buy the house."[23] The bankers claimed that only a few people who applied for the FHA mortgages wanted to buy a house outside the line.[24] But as Senator Hart put it, "To argue that in any event nobody wanted to get property beyond the line is sort of like saying no Irish applied and the fact that I had a sign up 'Irish may not apply' proves nothing."[25]

According to the 1970 census, the area inside the "red line" was at that time 53.8% black, compared to 6.4% outside the line.

The Real Estate Brokers

The BBURG program was not the only source of criticism. People claimed that the "red line" encouraged panic selling and speculation. And, indeed, the area was subjected to excessive "block busting" by the real estate agents. The exact number of real estate agencies in Mattapan was not known. The fact is that many real estate agencies began operating along Blue Hill Avenue. One estimate was that about one hundred brokers operated in the entire BBURG area.[26] It seems clear that the brokers tried to scare the residents into selling their houses and moving and that they succeeded.

Some reference to block busting could be found in the daily press during 1969. Yet, most articles at that time, such as that entitled "Mattapan Faces Up to a Crisis,"[27] dealt more with the racial change in general. The first time public attention was drawn directly to the issue of block busting was in the summer of 1971. Articles entitled "A Closer Look at the Issue of Block Busting" reported on the profits real estate agents were making in the area, including figures.[28]

The subject of the real estate activities was dealt with intensively at the Senate Subcommittee on Antitrust and Monopoly hearings cited above. Some brokers admitted buying property for a low price and reselling it for a much higher price (for example, buying a house for $11,500 and reselling it after five months for $20,000). Yet, as one broker claimed, "I do not see anything wrong. I think an investor improves the street. He goes in and fixes it up. The owners do not have the money or they just will not do it."[29] Although some of the brokers claimed that "they [the sellers] were glad to find a buyer, they wanted to sell and get out. They used to call me, I did not chase anybody,"[30] some of their tactics were revealed in the hearings. Brokers would send letters to Mattapan home owners saying, "We would like to extend our services to you. If you have considered selling your home, perhaps have tried without success, let us help you."[31] It was found that one broker sent out approximately 10,000 letters like this during the calendar year 1971.[32] Other brokers admitted calling people and offering them their services. One former resident testified, "Telephone calls by the realtors became a daily routine."[33]

Panic selling was not limited to the area inside the "red line," and some brokers testified that they "helped" people outside the line to sell their property. The real estate agents were of diverse backgrounds—Jews, blacks, and gentiles participated in block busting.[34]

Property Prices in Mattapan

One of the results of the real estate activities was that those who sold very often got a lower price for their house than they thought it was worth. Another source of discontent were the FHA appraisers, who, according to former residents, deliberately appraised the houses low. "In my opinion, the FHA created a ghetto by evaluating homes at their own price, so that BBURG could finance low income black families within their own established boundary lines."[35]

The Senate subcommittee dealt with the question of whether prices drop in a changing neighborhood. Although some studies indicated that property value does not inevitably drop in such a situation (Laurenti, 1960; Millen, 1973), the Boston bankers did not share this view. "I think it is absolutely inherent in the present relationship between whites and blacks, historically, and how soon it can be eliminated I cannot know. But at the moment, let us be realistic about it. If blacks move into white neighborhoods, it does tend to decrease value."[36] The reason is "the lesser price reflects anticipation of a lesser demand or of cheaper demand." The effect of the drop in property value is also felt in adjacent areas, according to the bankers. In 1970, 17% of the population in the area closest to the "red line" was already black.

This view expressed by the bankers was shared by the black residents themselves. One black resident bitterly remarked, "We know what is going to happen with blacks who put their life's savings down in Mattapan and try to turn around in three years and sell their homes. They are going to have to sell them under the cost of the property, the value which they bought them."[37]

No data is available on sale prices prior to the Senate sub-committee hearings. In the period from November, 1971, to December, 1972, the median price for a house in Mattapan was $22,210. About half of the property was sold for $20,000 to $24,900; 28.6% of the property was sold for less than $20,000; while 21.6% was sold for $25,000 and more.[38]

Although no data is available on the income level of the black families buying these houses, the BBURG ownership study indicated that 67% of all BBURG buyers earned more than $8,400 in 1971.[39]

Crime in Mattapan

The Roxbury riots in 1967 and 1968 seemed to have little impact on Mattapan proper, at least as far as one can judge from newspaper articles. Dorchester had begun changing earlier, and, as we have seen, this was accompanied by crime and the fear of crime. The newspapers referred to crimes in Dorchester in articles such as "Merchants on Blue Hill Avenue Dorchester Request Police Protection."[40] Yet, it was not until mid-1969 that attention was drawn to safety problems in Mattapan proper.

In July, 1969, the *Jewish Advocate* in an article, "Attack Mattapan Rabbi at Home," reported that acid was thrown into the face of Rabbi Zelermyer of Temple Beth Hillel on Morton Street (the northern border of Mattapan) by two black young-sters.[41] A short time later it was announced that "Temple Beth Hillel on Morton Street to be Relocated."[42] It seems now, that since this incident, full attention had been drawn to Mattapan proper. In the following months, stories appeared in the papers describing incidents of crime in Mattapan, especially attacks on elderly people. "Epidemic of Fear Grips Mattapan,"[43] was one of the headlines of these stories. It was reported that the state senator had asked for more police protection in the area. The crime rate, according to this article, increased in the first nine months of 1969 by 16.9%, compared to 12.1% in the city as a whole.[44]

The Jewish community at large began to pay attention to the Mattapan Jews. An *Advocate* editorial claimed that "The Jews of the changing neighborhood had been hurt many times, physi-cally by attack and emotionally by the feeling of sense of isolation for the abandonment of the Jewish community at large."[45] Let-ters to the editor appeared urging the Jewish organizations to do something about the Mattapan Jews. "The Jewish community in the Roxbury-Dorchester-Mattapan area is in my opinion worth preserving." Or, as a rabbi wrote, "We cannot just let the situa-tion remain as it is—remember 'all of Israel is responsible for one another.'"[46]

Another response was that of the Jewish Defense League (JDL), which announced its plans to patrol the area. It seems very clear that the Jewish community at large was divided around this issue. From letters to the *Jewish Advocate* one could learn that while some people denounced the JDL's tactics, others regarded it as the proper answer to the problem of the Mattapan Jews.

The Jewish organizations very strongly opposed the JDL and announced that "The Jewish Community Council agreed that only the police and not JDL can protect the elderly Jews."[47] Yet, on the other hand, it was announced that "JDL Begins Patrol in Mattapan."[48] (The area which was patrolled seemed to be, according to the papers, mainly north of Morton Street and less Mattapan proper.)

The Jewish organizations responded to the situation and to the various pressures by making efforts to "stabilize the neighborhood." It was announced that "a multiservice program designated by the CJP has been set up to meet the primary needs."[49] The Combined Jewish Philanthropies opened a drop-in center in December, 1969. The center moved to its location on Blue Hill Avenue in Mattapan in July, 1970.[50]

City officials, in addition to the Jewish organizations, also tried at that time to respond to the problems of Mattapan. It was announced that "Mayor White has directed a special task force to resolve the problems in the racially changing neighborhood."[51] One of the task force's recommendations was to increase police protection in the area. This recommendation was carried out, and in January, 1970, the "Subcommittee on Police-Community Relations reported that police protection had increased over the last few weeks, primarily because of an increase of officers in District Three Station."[52]

These measures, however, did not seem to have an impact on the crime rate in Mattapan. As a matter of fact, the opposite was true; as police statistics indicate, crime increased between 1969 and 1971 (see Table 7).

The rate of violent street crimes, that is, aggravated assaults and robberies, had risen tremendously in Mattapan during the two years for which statistics are available. Although the offense rate in general was lower in Mattapan than in Boston (50.28 per 1,000 for Mattapan compared to 67.76 in Boston in 1971), the robbery rate was higher that year in Mattapan (10.18 compared to 7.51 in Boston). It seems clear that the *increase* of violent crimes was much higher in Mattapan than in Boston.

Property crimes were lower in Mattapan than in Boston, and auto thefts and nonresidential burglaries even decreased in the

TABLE 7

Crime Rates in Mattapan and Boston, 1969-1971

(Rates per 1000 Persons)

Type of Crime	Mattapan			Boston			Percentage Change (1969-1971)	
	1969	1970	1971	1969	1970	1971	Mattapan	Boston
Aggravated Assaults	0.92	1.43	2.25	2.39	2.59	3.05	144.6	28.1
Robberies	3.84	7.62	10.18	4.77	5.41	7.51	165.1	57.4
Auto Thefts	17.70	16.26	15.29	24.21	24.35	25.86	−15.8	6.8
Non residential Burglaries	3.48	2.92	2.61	5.44	4.93	5.46	−33.3	0.4
Residential Burglaries	11.40	9.97	11.58	8.80	10.96	14.63	1.0	66.2
Larceny	4.76	8.03	6.85	14.67	19.59	19.55	43.9	32.6

Source: "Crime in Boston 1969–71," The Mayor's Office of Justice Administration, Tables 7–12, pp. 23–28.

years 1969 through 1971. The rate of residential burglaries in 1969 was higher for Mattapan than for the city, decreased in 1970, and increased again in 1971. At that time residential burglaries increased in Boston, and the rate for the city in 1971 was higher than for Mattapan.

The important facts of these figures are no doubt the high rate of increase in violent street crimes. These are the types of crimes which are most visible, which people talk about and hear about, which are reported by the media, and which seem to account for headlines such as "Terror Despair Grips Mattapan Jews."[53] It is also important to remember that the rate of violent crimes in Mattapan is much higher than in places like Brookline (a suburban town on the western border of Boston with a large Jewish community), Milton (a suburban town on the southern border of Boston adjacent to Mattapan), and Newton (again, a suburb west of Boston with a large Jewish community), which serve as reference points for the Jewish resident of Mattapan.

The Schools

One of the major "problems" of Mattapan was connected with the racial change in the schools, mainly the Lewenberg Junior High School. Perhaps more than any other issue, the change in the school focused attention on the problem of the integrated neighborhood, before the neighborhood actually changed. As a result of open enrollment, black students were bused into the Lewenberg school, and the school began to change a long time before blacks moved into the area. In a period of eight years the school's student body changed from almost all white to almost all black (see Table 8).

The "tipping point" of the school seemed to be between the years 1967–68 and 1968–69, when the percentage of black students increased by 31%. In 1968–69, 50% of the white students living in the area were transferred to other schools.[54]

Newspaper articles reported on the rate of racial change in

TABLE 8
Percentage of Black Students in the Lewenberg Junior High School

Year	Percent
1964–65	10
1965–66	25
1966–67	34
1967–68	45
1968–69	76
1969–70	86
1970–71	93
1971–72	95

Source: Boston School Committee, 1972.

the school quite often, relating the school problems to the change. The general assumption was that

> . . . the quality of education in the Solomon Lewenberg Junior High School and in several of the elementary schools has decreased. The influx of children from low income families with poor preparation and home background has put a strain on the teachers. Poor students slow down all the students and discipline problems disrupt the classes.[55]

In January, 1970, the Mayor's Task Force even recommended closing down the Lewenberg Junior High School "in order to draw attention of public officials to the discipline problems and the deplorable physical conditions."[56] The same article mentioned that none of the staff was black.

Some of the former Mattapan residents who testified in the Senate hearings referred to the schools. "The tremendous rise in crime and the terrorism in the local schools increased our fears."[57] It was generally assumed that many parents left the area because of the schools. From the 1970 census it seems that the area around the school was the first to change. In 1970, 66.6% of the population in this area was already black.

Later articles dealing with the Lewenberg school reported

that the atmosphere in the school had changed. "Today new methods of teaching are being implemented and there is hope. The kids, the teachers and the community have a different attitude, it is positive."[58] Yet, it is clear that racial balance had not been achieved and that the school changed from all white to all black in eight years.

Mattapan after the Senate Subcommittee Hearings

Mattapan remained in the news even after the hearings. The real estate activities quieted down for several months, but sales did not stop. The brokers apparently became somewhat more cautious, and the FHA more active in stopping their illegal activities. In April, 1972, the papers announced that "US May Act Against 2 Real Estate Firms."[59]

The banks became reluctant to give FHA mortgages, and for a short period after the hearings, sales in the area dropped. After a while, however, the sales resumed, and between November, 1971, and December, 1972, 392 properties were sold in Mattapan proper.[60] Only 17% of the sales were inside the "red line"; all the others were outside. The banks apparently extended the line to the whole Mattapan area. This meant that blacks began moving in sizable numbers toward the southern sections of the area. This is apparent when one examines the type of housing sold in the last year (1972). Whereas previous to the Senate hearings most of the sales were, according to the bankers, of two- and three-family houses, in the later periods over half of the sales were single-family homes. Of the 392 houses sold in Mattapan between November, 1971, and December, 1972, 53% were single homes, 27% were two family houses, and only 17% of the houses sold were three-family houses or larger.[61]

Although no statistics are available, it seems that the blacks, who comprised only 5.2% of the population of census tract 1010 in 1970, constituted in 1973 a large portion of the population of this section. The movement of blacks has a distinctive pattern, going from north to south.

Recently blacks began moving onto the predominantly non-Jewish streets on the southern border of Mattapan. At the beginning the change hit only the Jewish area, but as a Catholic priest admitted, "As soon as they started crossing Walk Hill Street, we began losing some parishioners."[62] The priest began a campaign against panic selling, distributing signs reading, "Mine not for sale."[63]

Crime in the area continues to make headlines, and articles such as "Holdups turn Mattapan into Plywood City,"[64] appear quite often. A recent incident reported the unfortunate murder of an elderly Jewish man in his Mattapan apartment.[65]

Some neighborhood groups, such as "The Mattapan Board of Trade," are still trying to preserve the area, at least by preventing deterioration of the shopping center. Yet, whatever the results of efforts like this are likely to be, the white exodus continues, and the percentage of blacks increases.

Summary

The process of racial change in Mattapan has been in many respects similar to that of other neighborhoods in various cities. First, Mattapan is located on the border of the existing black community. The growth of the black population in Boston and the displacement of many people because of urban renewal in the central city neighborhoods has inevitably resulted in the expansion of the black neighborhoods. As we have seen, adjacent Dorchester began changing long before Mattapan did, and the migration trend of the black population was already directed toward this neighborhood.

Second, the age structure of the white population of Mattapan was typical of that of a changing neighborhood. Young families started moving out to the suburbs in the 1950's and

1960's, and those who remained in the area were to a large extent elderly people. Thus, Mattapan had become an aging community even before the blacks started to move into the neighborhood.

Third, the availability of a good, fairly inexpensive housing stock made the area attractive for black families looking for a home. As we have seen, Mattapan (in contrast to other changing neighborhoods) has a relatively high percentage of new housing units built in the 1950's and 1960's. The out-migration of whites made the homes available to the incoming blacks.

Yet, this "normal" process of racial transition, so typical of many American cities, was hastened by several external factors. Although it is impossible to judge the impact of these factors on the process of change, they seem to be important. The racial change of the school as a result of an open-enrollment policy contributed to the out-migration of families with children. The BBURG program, which enabled black families to buy homes with low down-payments and easy mortgage terms in this area only, added to the process of rapid racial transition. This process was accompanied by intensive real estate activities and by panic selling. The rise in crime rates was another factor contributing to the out-migration of the white population.

As a result of racial transition, the population of Mattapan seems to consist of small, elderly white families, on the one hand, and young, quite large black families on the other.

Not much was left of the Jewish community of Mattapan when I started this study. In the summer of 1972, while I was doing the fieldwork, it was estimated that less than 2,500 Jews, which amounted to about 1,300 family units, still lived in the area.[66] Most Jews lived in the southern part of Mattapan. Only about 100 Jewish family units remained inside the "red line," which was the core of Jewish Mattapan in the past. Thus, due to the exodus of the Jewish people, the Jewish population of Mattapan decreased from 10,000 in 1968 to less than 2,500 in 1972.

NOTES

1 Report on The Mattapan Organization by Mark Israel, May, 1968.

2 No further distinction on the year the structure was built is given for black households.

3 Jewish Community Council of Metropolitan Boston, Annual Report 1966–1967, June 1, 1967, p. 3.

4 *The Boston Globe*, February 7, 1967.

5 Report on The Mattapan Organization by Mark Israel, May, 1968.

6 *The Boston Globe*, February 7, 1967.

7 *Ibid.*

8 Jewish Community Council of Metropolitan Boston, Annual Report, 1966–1967, June 1, 1967, p. 5.

9 Report on The Mattapan Organization by Mark Israel, May, 1968, p. 1.

10 *Boston Herald Traveler*, November 28, 1969.

11 *Ibid.*

12 Testimony of Joseph H. Bacheller, Jr., "Competition in Real Estate and Mortgage Lending." Hearings before the Subcommittee on Antitrust and Monopoly of the Committee on the Judiciary. U.S. Senate, 92 congress, second session, Part 1, Boston, September 13, 14 and 15, 1971, p. 255.

13 Ibid.

14 Testimony of Mr. Erickson, Subcommittee on Antitrust and Monopoly, *op. cit.*, p. 284.

15 "Crisis in Mattapan," *The Boston Globe*, April 4, 1972.

16 Testimony of Joseph Bacheller, Subcommittee on Antitrust and Monopoly, *op. cit.*, p. 291.

17 Jewish Community Council of Metropolitan Boston, Annual Report 1966–1967, June 1, 1967, p. 3.

18 In the *New York Times* of January 21, 1973, an article entitled, "Racial Change Slashes Values and Produces Bargains," describes the transition of a neighborhood in Philadelphia from Jewish to black.

19 Testimony of Mrs. Bernstein before the Subcommittee on Antitrust and Monopoly, *op. cit.*, p. 74.

20 Testimony of Walter Smart before the Subcommittee on Antitrust and Monopoly, *op. cit.*, pp. 121–123.

21 "A Home Ownership Survey, a Report on the Boston Banks Urban Renewal Group," prepared for the Model City Administration by Rachel G. Bratt, January, 1972, Appendix B, Table 6.

22 Mrs. Barbara Shanon of Dorchester testified that when she read about the possibility of an FHA mortgage in the papers, she called several real estate brokers, but they never returned her calls. (Subcommittee on Antitrust and Monopoly, *op. cit.*, p. 102.)

23 "A Home Ownership Survey," *op. cit.*, p. 21.

24 Testimony of Joseph Bacheller, Subcommittee on Antitrust and Monopoly, *op. cit.*, p. 262.

25 Chairman, Subcommittee on Antitrust and Monopoly, *op. cit.*, p. 263.

26 Testimony of Mr. Chumbris, Subcommittee on Antitrust and Monopoly, *op. cit.*, p. 189.

27 *The Boston Herald Traveler*, January 5, 1969.

28 *The Boston Globe*, June 3, 1971.

29 Testimony of Mr. Medverd, Subcommittee on Antitrust and Monopoly, *op. cit.*, p. 139.

30 *Ibid.*

31 Subcommittee on Antitrust and Monopoly, *op. cit.*, pp. 163-164.

32 *Ibid.*

33 Testimony of Mrs. Bernstein, Subcommittee on Antitrust and Monopoly, *op. cit.*, p. 73.

34 It was impossible to find out the number of brokers in the area and their division by ethnic background because some were unlisted and operated out of their homes.

35 Testimony of Mrs. Bernstein, *op. cit.*, p. 75.

36 Testimony of Joseph Bacheller, Subcommittee on Antitrust and Monopoly, *op. cit.*, p. 292.

37 Testimony of Mr. Fortes of the Mattapan Block Association, Subcommittee on Antitrust and Monopoly, *op. cit.*, p. 337.

38 According to the Metropolitan Mortgage cards, November 10, 1971, to December 27, 1972.

39 "A Home Ownership Survey," *op. cit.*, p. 27.

40 *The Boston Herald Traveler*, October 10, 1968.

41 *The Jewish Advocate*, July 25, 1969.

42 *The Jewish Advocate*, August 21, 1969.

43 *The Boston Herald Traveler*, November 24, 1969.

44 *The Boston Globe*, November 25, 1969.

45 *The Jewish Advocate*, July 10, 1969.

46 *The Jewish Advocate*, July 31, 1969.

47 *The Boston Herald Traveler*, November 24, 1969.

48 *The Boston Globe*, December 1, 1969.

49 *The Boston Globe*, November 19, 1969.

50 After I finished this study, the drop-in center moved to a still white area on the edge of Mattapan.

51 *The Boston Globe*, November 25, 1969.

52 *The Boston Globe*, January 21, 1970.

53 *The Boston Globe*, November 25, 1969.

54 Boston School Committee, 1972.

55 Jewish Community Council of Metropolitan Boston, Annual Report 1966–1967, June 1, 1967, p. 5.

56 *The Boston Globe*, January 21, 1970.

57 Testimony of Mrs. Bernstein, Subcommittee on Antitrust and Monopoly, *op. cit.*, p. 75.

58 *The Boston Globe*, January 21, 1970.

59 *The Boston Globe*, April 25, 1972.

60 It is impossible to tell how many buyers applied for mortgages before the hearings.

61 Metropolitan Mortgage cards, November 10, 1971—December 27, 1972.

62 *The Boston Globe*, April 6, 1972.

63 According to the then local priest, the parish lost about 400 of its 1,400 families in a period of 3 to 4 years. There is a slow out-migration of white Catholics, although it is far less rapid than the Jewish exodus. From the information I gathered it seems that the area around the church remained pretty much white; blacks and white Catholics, in most cases, do not live on the same streets.

One of the interesting questions is why did the Jewish people move out of Mattapan much faster than the Catholics? It would be impossible to answer this question without studying the non-Jewish whites in the area. One of the possible explanations, according to the priest, is that the Catholics were better organized than the Jews and had a stronger local leadership. Also, the parochial school was an important reason for staying in the area. One should keep in mind, however, that it was much easier to get a mortgage when the Jews started moving out of Mattapan than it has been in recent years when the non-Jewish whites have begun to move out. The mortgage market has since become fairly tight, and the banks are reluctant to give mortgages, particularly in transitional areas.

64 *The Boston Globe*, May 4, 1972.

65 *The Boston Globe*, March 21, 1973.

66 A rough count of the Jewish people of Mattapan was carried out by the CJP in August–September, 1972. Although it by no means reflects the precise number of Jews living in the area at that time, it might serve as a more or less fair estimate.

About 500 families were relocated from Dorchester and Mattapan by the Jewish Family and Children Service from mid-1970 to the end of 1971. Most people, however, left on their own, without help.

CHAPTER THREE

The Research Method

This study is based mainly on open-ended interviews with 100 Jewish people in Mattapan. Additional data on the neighborhood was collected from the census, police and school statistics, the mortgage bureau, newspaper articles, and various documents such as those of the Senate subcommittee hearings in Boston. I also interviewed members of Jewish and non-Jewish service organizations, city and government employees dealing with the area, the local police, the parish priest, the rabbi, and a few black community leaders.

I began the study in December, 1971, first gathering all of the background information. From April to August, 1972, I conducted interviews with the Jewish residents. During this period I visited the neighborhood daily, spending most of my time there. I interviewed during various hours of the day and evening, including weekends.

The Research Procedure

I carried out the study from beginning to end, collecting and analyzing my own data. No doubt this fact had a strong impact on the direction and even on the quality of the study. Very often I wondered how the work would have come out had I analyzed someone else's data or if someone else had written up the material I collected.

Doing a study from the beginning to the end has advantages and disadvantages, and I am aware of both. Yet, in this particular setting of a changing neighborhood, it seems to me that the advantages are greater than the disadvantages. The entire study is dominated to a large extent by the fact that Mattapan is a changing neighborhood, with all the research problems connected with this fact. I would never have understood what it is like to live in a changing area without having spent a great deal of time in Mattapan. I would never have imagined the extent to which people's lives are dominated by fear without having been exposed to it myself.

In this respect, my experience in the field served as a very valuable source of data. In a way I learned more from my observations than from the interviews.

Doing Fieldwork in the Neighborhood

I began studying the Jewish people in Mattapan without thinking that I was doing a study in a "dangerous area," or that I had to be more cautious than in any other place. I read newspaper articles describing the holdups and bag snatching in Mattapan, but paid little attention to them. I was warned by members of the service organizations and by city employees not to walk on the streets and to be careful. Every time I made an appointment with any of them our conversation would end with the words, "I don't want you to come after dark" (it was in the winter). The rabbi who at that time still lived in the area expressed his concern when I told him I would be walking from the bus stop to his house. The manager of the Little City Hall disapproved when I walked from her office to the public library, a five-minute walk. I paid little attention to all these warnings, and to be honest, was even slightly amused that everyone was so concerned about my safety.

At first glimpse Blue Hill Avenue did not look like a danger-ous area. True, the boarded-up stores made a depressing impres-sion on me, but I could not find any relationship between the sight of them and my personal safety.

The first days in the field were discouraging, and at some point I half thought of giving up the whole study. It became clear to me that this neighborhood was not what I had imagined. After all, perhaps there was some truth in the stories of the community workers.

The most disturbing aspect for me concerned the fact that I walked in the area. Not having a car during the first two weeks, I used public transportation. Since I could not reach the side streets by bus, I began walking along them. As it turned out one April morning, I was the only human being on the streets. After a while I had a funny feeling that something might be wrong. The surroundings ceased to be "normal" for me. I paid attention to each noise, imagined hearing footsteps behind me, and felt an uneasiness slowly creeping over me. Of course the children were at school and working people were not around, but it was an extremely uncomfortable feeling to be the only person on the streets. After several days like this, I was glad to be able to drive around in a car.

I learned later that the neighborhood is not totally one of deserted streets. There are still some "good" streets in the area where one can see people walking. These are, however, small enclaves at the southern end of Mattapan.

My only company on the deserted streets were the dogs that walked around freely. I was always accompanied by a couple of large dogs. The area was full of them, and "Beware of Dog" signs were posted on many houses. I have never seen so many dogs in my life. The entrances to the old apartment buildings were especially scary. I opened front doors never knowing if I would find a big dog sitting there staring at me. The only thing I could think of was to act normally and not to show an animal how frightened I was. I tried to ignore them, but sometimes they would bark so that I would have to leave a building without being able to check the mailbox. In other instances when I rang an apartment bell, I would hear a dog barking wildly. It usually took about ten minutes for the animal to quiet down so I could finally enter the apartment.

Even with a car I felt that I was in an "abnormal" situation in the sense that occurrences to which I would not pay attention in any other setting suddenly became sources of anxiety and insecurity (Goffman, 1971). In one of the first weeks while I was checking some names on the front of a new apartment building, the mailman asked me in a suspicious voice, "Whom are you looking for?" I was alarmed, and my first reaction was to tell him to mind his own business. Nevertheless, I told him for whom I was looking and then asked him why he had to know. He explained that the post office and the police were instructed to ask any stranger what he was looking for. Behavior which in any other place would be regarded as normal was seen there as suspicious.

I always had the feeling that people were spying on me. I would drive slowly down a street and see people looking at me from their windows. Very often when I parked my car and checked an address, somebody would ask, "What are you looking for?" I almost felt as if I had to apologize for wandering around in the area, and this feeling was exaggerated when I passed the courtyard of the large apartment complex. My situation was a real dilemma; I hated to walk alone, but I also hated to meet people who might ask me for explanations. I was extremely sensitive to this, and that made the feeling of unpleasantness even stronger.

Indicators of a Changing Neighborhood

Walking and even driving through Mattapan was an enlightening experience in itself. As I mentioned before, most of the neighborhood looked like a pleasant suburban area, very different from the slum one would have expected in a changing neighborhood. Driving through the small streets I would sometimes see a man painting a house or mowing a lawn.

Many things, however, indicated that Mattapan was a changing neighborhood. One could see many "for sale" signs on the one- and two-family houses, and "vacancies" on the apartment buildings. Trucks were always parked on the streets, unloading and loading furniture. It was clear that people were moving. On some small houses one could see signs indicating "mine not for sale," but even they made me feel uneasy. Something was wrong with the area if people had to announce their intentions to stay there.

It was quite clear that the area was in the process of racial change. I felt very much out of place driving through the streets in the northern part of Mattapan, where only a few white people lived. Driving through the streets on a July morning, with all the black children and their mothers watching them from time to time from the porches, made me very conscious of the fact that I was white. I had the same strange feeling when I was the only white person on the bus, or when I walked through the First National supermarket. The clientele and some of the employees were black; I counted three white customers. I could later understand what people meant when they said, "We don't belong here any more; we are the odds now."

"Normal" Behavior

Looking back, my actions during this period seem strange to me now, if not ridiculous. At the time, however, my behavior seemed to me perfectly normal. During the four months I interviewed daily in the area I always expected something to happen to me. I expected that I would be mugged or beaten or at least held up. Surprisingly, nothing happened; my car was not stolen and nobody tried to bother me.

The feeling of insecurity was of course reinforced by the stories I heard from people and by the way they reacted toward me. I remember the reaction of those who heard I went about on foot. I was once talking to a partially deaf man who preferred that I interview his wife, who was not at home. I explained to him that I would walk around and come back later. When I finally found the woman at home, she was hysterical, unable to understand how her husband could have let me walk around.

I cannot recall getting so much advice concerning my behavior as I did in Mattapan. People warned me, told me what to do and what not to do, where to drive, and so forth. Usually when people saw my handbag they would say, "Huhhh, you carry a bag. You shouldn't carry a bag. If I were you, I wouldn't carry a bag!" Even the policeman in front of the public library told me I should not carry a bag. His advice was to pin the money inside my dress.

People would ask me if I locked my car, and then they would repeat, "Are you sure you locked it?" Of course, by then I was not sure anymore and was surprised each time I found my car untouched. Another piece of advice was: "Lock your car when you are driving up Blue Hill Avenue. Shut your windows." I found myself pushing down the buttons on the car doors, although I never do it anywhere else. When I had to stop at the red light on one of the "bad" streets, I always instinctively closed the windows, despite the heat.

I interviewed often in the evenings because I also wanted to include in the study those who worked during the day. One night, around 8:15, a woman began nagging her husband, "Let her go, it's getting dark." The man, however, still had a lot to tell me and did not want me to go. When I finally left the house it was completely dark. I drove up Blue Hill Avenue, which was well lit with neon lights, but nobody was on the street. My car was locked, my windows closed, and I could hear my heart beating.

One afternoon I parked my car on a street on which only a few Jews lived. I looked for one family that no longer lived there and then started off to another address. As I knew the distance was only a five-minute walk, I left my car. When I finished the interview the woman suggested that she go downstairs with me to the gate of her house and stand there until I reached my car. She said, "You parked so far; I wouldn't do it if I were you. I park in front of the house." I tried to dismiss the issue, but while I was walking toward the car, knowing she was looking after me, I suddenly got scared. I imagined boys running after me and snatching my bag. When I finally reached my car I noticed I was sweating all over. The knowledge that the woman was watching me made me realize that something was wrong, that I must be careful, that it was dangerous to walk on this street.

It was depressing to stop at one of the stores along Blue Hill Avenue. Once I visited one of the three Jewish butchers left on the Avenue. He was located in a building with eight other stores, most of them boarded up. On one side was a cocktail lounge and on the other a billiard room. Some black youngsters were walking around, staring at me sitting in the car. I had $30 with me. Suddenly I thought perhaps it would be better to leave the money in the car and just carry my empty bag with me. I was tempted to do so, but decided otherwise. I was even angry with myself—why do I have to behave in such a peculiar way just because two black teenagers are looking at me?

I left the car and started toward the butcher. There was a lot of garbage and several empty cans on the sidewalk. The butcher's door was locked, and he stayed inside, looking at me for a long moment before deciding to open the door. Apparently new white customers did not visit him any more. I explained what I was doing in the area while he continued to cut his meat. He had been there for over twenty years and could not afford to move because the rents elsewhere were much higher. "But when you

have to lock your door, it's no good any more." He had been held
up, but refused to discuss it with me. When I left, he said,
"Watch your bag. They are *chappen* [snatching] them!" I was
glad to be back in my car.

After experiencing all of this, I realized how infectious the
whole atmosphere of the neighborhood was. Because I was
exposed to it myself, I was able to empathize with the people and
understand them better.

Entering People's Homes

I began interviewing the Jewish population in April, 1972.
Armed with a list of Jewish-sounding names taken from the 1972
voting registration lists, and with a detailed map of the area, I
started knocking on doors. I relied completely on my past experience with interviewing and did not give a second thought to the
fact that a study in such an area might be different. However, it
was totally unique in my experience.

The most serious problem I had in my fieldwork was that
people did not at first let me into their homes. I would ring a bell
or knock on a door and hear somebody ask, "Who is it?" Sometimes I would only hear a voice, not knowing where it came from.
Looking up and yelling into the air, I would explain who I was. I
felt ridiculous, but I had no other choice. In the old apartment
buildings without intercommunication devices, people sometimes talked to me from behind closed doors. In the one- or two-
family houses I would usually hear chains and locks opening and
see a face peek out through the window of the inside door.

I tried to convince people of my good intentions, telling them
that I was a Harvard student doing a study among the Jews in
Mattapan. To win their confidence I said I was Jewish and from
Israel (which I am). On some occasions I even said a few words in
my very bad and broken Yiddish. All of this usually made very
little impression on the people. I was a stranger and strangers

were not allowed in their homes. Some would not even see me, and we carried on the "conversation" through locked doors. Even the fact that I was an Israeli did not help much; one woman called out beyond a closed door that she had already contributed. I could not convince her that I did not want a donation. In some cases, mainly in the one-family houses, people felt sorry for me and let me in, but they were exceptions. After wandering in the area for several days, I succeeded in getting eight interviews— and about fifty refusals.

After my unsuccessful attempts to interview people by simply knocking on doors, I sent out letters explaining who I was and describing the purpose of the study. There is no doubt that the letters helped. Many people knew who I was, and some even expected me; others were more cautious. A few people denied getting the letter, even after I showed them a copy of it. Others asked, "Which letter?" and only after seeing a copy admitted having received it. One lady called her social worker after receiving my letter, and the social worker confirmed that I was "O.K." Some thought I was a real estate agent, despite my letter, and it was difficult to convince them otherwise. Others asked for my credentials even after letting me in.

Gaining entry to new apartment buildings presented a greater problem since I had to identify myself through the intercom. It was difficult for me to convince people that I was harmless without their seeing me. One "discussion" went like this: "Are you a girl? Are you Jewish? Are you from Israel?—I'm sorry, I don't let anybody I don't know in." I almost gave up but then suggested that the woman come downstairs and look at me. After that she let me in and even apologized for being so suspicious.

In some cases when people let me in, I entered without any idea of where I was going. This was extremely unpleasant in old apartment buildings. Once I heard a buzzer, opened the front door, and began climbing the spiral staircase in the darkness. There were no names on the apartment doors, and I had no idea where the people I was looking for lived. Suddenly, when I reached the last floor, a door opened a little and a woman asked, "Is it you?" and let me in.

In some cases I was not asked to come in. People would come down and open the door a little behind the chain. Some remained standing inside, talking to me from behind a screen door. It was uncomfortable to interview people while I was standing outside. A few warmed up and let me in after a while. One man stood in front of his one-family house and said, "There is nothing to tell; the area is changing and that's it." After ten minutes he invited me to come in and offered me some coffee. Two and a half hours later it was hard for me to leave the house.

In spite of the letters, some people (thirty-seven) refused to talk with me. In a few cases they did not even bother to answer the door, although I was sure they were at home. Some said they were not interested or that they did not want to get involved. "I don't understand what that has to do with me. There are a few Jewish people around here. I don't know anybody, and nobody bothers me." Others called out that they did not have time and that was it. Doors were slammed in my face, intercom connections were broken. I even got an angry letter advising me to do my social studies elsewhere.

These refusals made me angry. Yet, most of the time I felt sorry for the people who refused to talk with me. One time an elderly woman opened her door a little behind the chain and, trembling all over, said, "I'm sorry, my daughter told me not to talk with anybody." Another time an elderly man opened his door and said, "I'm sorry, I don't want to comment on this subject. I have no opinion, and even if I had, they [the politicians] decide and do what they want. . . . To tell you the truth, I'm afraid to talk." Once a woman opened a small window, looked at me, and said, "I'm sorry, I don't let strangers in." I tried to explain, showed her a copy of the letter, presented my student's card— but nothing helped.

The deserted streets and people refusing to let me into their homes gave me perhaps the most important clues to understanding what the neighborhood was like. I suddenly realized how painful the whole situation was. I never before imagined how frightened and suspicious people could be. After seeing and experiencing the area, I could understand much more clearly what people meant when they said, "You cannot walk here anymore" or "You are afraid of your own shadow."

I had not thought of this aspect beforehand, but after the first few days in the field, I began paying special attention to the way people opened their doors and addressed themselves to me. I saw in their behavior an important indication of their reaction toward a stranger.

My experience in the field also gave me some ideas about which questions to ask. I asked people whether they walked on the streets, how they protected themselves when they went out, what safety devices they had (including dogs), and if they let strangers into their houses. The whole subject of fear and security became an important dimension in the study, partly because I was exposed to these problems myself.

The Interviewing Process

As I already mentioned, the interviews were open-ended and unstructured; I did not use any questionnaire. When I began interviewing I had only a vague idea of the important issues and was able to ask only very general questions. I did not know exactly what questions I was going to ask. I wanted to understand what it was like for Jewish people to live in a racially changing neighborhood. Since most studies dealing with the subject concentrate more on the reasons for residential change than on the dynamic aspects of living in such a community, they were of little help. In this respect this study is to a large extent exploratory.

My experience in the field gave me a most important insight into what it was like to live in such a community. But of course I learned a great deal more through the interviewing process. The more people I interviewed, the more I learned what the important issues were in this situation and the better able I was to ask specific questions. Yet, even then I found that I was getting better data when I let people talk freely and describe the situation rather than direct them to specific issues. I would usually ask general questions, let people talk, and only if I did not get the information I wanted would I be more direct and specific.

A question such as "How did you feel the neighborhood was changing?" brought a sequence of answers. People would in general describe the process in length. Only by asking such a broad question did I realize, for instance, that people distinguish between change in their immediate vicinity and change in the whole area. The question of change in the person's life would bring forward the issue of fear and safety on one hand and that of getting used to black people on the other.

Since I had no fixed interviewing schedule, the sequence of the questions was dependent on the people as well as on myself. (For a general list of questions, see the Appendix.) Very often when I interviewed more than one member of a family, the interview turned into a lively discussion. In nonstandardized interviews such as those I carried out with the Jewish people of Mattapan, the length and even quality of the interviews varied from one person to another. I was often asked how long the interview was going to last, but was unable to answer. They took from three-quarters of an hour to three hours; most interviews lasted between two and three hours. Interestingly, some of the longest interviews were with people who claimed they had very little time.

In this kind of interview the quality depends to a large extent on the interaction between the interviewer and the interviewee. I was very much aware of the fact that some interviews were better than others. I tried to discover which were my best interviews, but I could not find a pattern. I had some good interviews with men and with women, with single people and with couples, with older people and with younger ones. Some people liked me better than others and that, of course, had an impact on the quality of data I was getting. I was once in a very delicate situation with an old couple. The man liked me and wanted to talk, but it was obvious that his wife disliked me. She was constantly sweeping the floor under my chair, making remarks about how busy they were, and being generally unfriendly. It was difficult to interview in a situation like that, and after an hour she finally drove me out of the apartment.

Aside from the fact that I did not know exactly what to ask, there was another reason that the interviews were open-ended and unstructured. Even if I had had a list of specific questions, it would have been impossible to approach most of the people with a questionnaire. My initial idea was to use a tape recorder or at least take notes during a conversation. However, after a few interviews I learned that it would be impossible to carry them out this way. People simply would not talk if I tried to write anything down.

In spite of my letter they were suspicious about what I was going to do with the information. Some asked me if I was a reporter or even a real estate agent, and I had to convince them repeatedly that I was just a student. Most emphasized that they did not want to be quoted and also wanted to be sure that the information was really confidential, as I had said in my letter. One woman even came running to my car a few moments after our interview was over and asked if I was hiding a tape recorder somewhere. The only way I could convince people that I did not intend to misuse the information they gave me or refer to any individual was to talk with them without taking notes. The result was that I conducted very free conversations with people. I did not have to concentrate on writing and was able to talk with them without any interruption.

On the other hand, it was difficult to memorize all that people told me, especially since most of the interviews were so long. I tried to record the interviews as precisely as possible, but

sometimes I could not remember all the details. At the beginning
it was difficult, but the more people I interviewed, the more I got
used to this method. Apparently, human memory is better than I
was ready to admit. Reading the interviews a few months later it
seemed obvious to me that I wrote down what the people said, in
their language, but I also realized that because the interviews
were recorded from memory, the quotes I used were not always
accurate.

The Problem of Involvement

One of the factors which helped me memorize what people
said was my deep involvement in the situation. When I began, I
did not realize how involved I would become. I soon discovered
that it was impossible to carry out a study like this in a detached,
professional manner, for the people I was studying were in a
painful situation.

I felt that people responded to me because I was sympathetic
with them. Although they realized that I was unable to help them
in any way, the opportunity to discuss their problems was often in
itself rewarding. Sometimes it was hard for me to take all this. I
almost "lived" with the stories during the four months of the
fieldwork. Days after I had interviewed a person I would suddenly
remember that I had forgotten to write down something he told
me. The data I collected was always on my mind, and it was a
heavy burden.

I sometimes asked myself whether I was doing the right thing
and whether I should indulge in a study in this area. People very
often asked me why I was doing this study, if I came from the
Jewish Philanthropies, and what good would it do in Mattapan. I
had to admit that I was only doing a study for my own purposes
and that I was unable to help them. I felt almost guilty when
people came up with these questions. In the case of one old
couple I interviewed, the man was blind and the woman very

frightened. They were the only whites among six black families in the house, and they were waiting desperately for the Jewish organizations to find them another apartment. The woman kept asking, "Why do I have to answer all these questions when you cannot help us?" At that moment it seemed to me senseless to interview her.

Interviewing old people was sometimes a hard task. Two-thirds of the people I interviewed were over sixty years old. Some were lonely, others were sick. A few had lost their husbands or wives recently and were miserable. I had to listen patiently to all kinds of stories, hear their troubles, and even admire photographs of their grandchildren. Some cried, and I did not know what to do. These were extremely embarrassing moments. Some described their ailments in detail, which was difficult to listen to. A seventy-five-year-old woman told me about her inflammatory arthritis and added, "If you could only see my toes!" I really felt sick at that moment.

My deep involvement in the situation often bothered me. In addition to the fact that it created an emotional strain, I was worried that I was getting a distorted picture. I suspected that I was seeing things too much through the eyes of the people and that I would not be able to properly analyze the data. Yet the fact that I was hearing the same stories more or less repeatedly convinced me that I was collecting reliable data.

Since I did the research from beginning to end, the entire study acquired a human dimension which was particularly gratifying from my point of view. I was dealing with real people, not just with stories. Although I analyzed the data about six months after collecting it, I recognized, and even visualized, the people while reading their interviews. Yet this same fact made the writing difficult. I wanted to summarize all that I heard and felt and knew. This "personal" relationship to the data made the task of choosing between the appropriate quotations, for instance, a hard one.

The main disadvantage of doing a complete study like this is

that it is difficult to reach a level of detachment from the data
without which it is impossible to analyze the material. There is
no doubt that a very deep involvement prevents a researcher
from presenting the data in its proper perspective. Despite my
doubts regarding the results of my involvement, I do not see any
other way of interviewing in a situation like that in Mattapan.
Perhaps the balance between the impact of involvement and the
necessary detachment can be reached when enough time passes
between the interviewing and the analysis of the data. When I
finished interviewing I was eager to begin writing up the material,
lest I should forget many important things. Yet now I think that
the longer the time between the two stages, the easier it would be
to analyze the data.

The Impact of Being a Stranger

I was very much aware of the fact that people let me into
their homes and talked to me the way they did because I was a
Jewish woman; I doubt if I would have gotten the same information had I not been. Often people used phrases such as "Between
you and me, our Jewish people, God bless them . . ." However,
aside from being a Jewish woman, I was also from another
country. Doing fieldwork in a different culture causes various
problems, the most obvious one being that of the language.
People sometimes used English words that I had never heard
before. I would write them down immediately after the interview
and check them later with the dictionary. Interviewing in a
foreign language is an additional cause of fatigue and strain.

On the other hand, I found that being a foreigner was also a
big advantage in this study. Many people I interviewed were not
fully "Americanized." Some were born abroad, and even though
they had been in this country for many years, they still spoke with
an accent. I was foreign born too, and in a way they felt a sympa-
thy toward me. This feeling was reinforced by the fact that I came

from Israel. I represented for many of them (despite my will) the "ideal" type of Jew—the one who fights back.

Another advantage of being a stranger was that I could ask embarrassing questions such as "What is wrong with living among blacks?" with the pretext of being unfamiliar with the situation. By the same token, I was able to avoid unpleasant arguments. I was dealing with the delicate subject of relations between two minority groups, and people sometimes wanted to hear my opinion. One man asked me angrily, "You are asking me questions, but you haven't committed yourself yet—are you for the Jews or for the blacks?" I was able to dismiss the question with the excuse of not being familiar enough with the situation.

Inevitably one of the major topics of an interview in a racially changing neighborhood is the attitudes of the Jewish people toward the blacks. At the beginning I resented the way people talked about the blacks, and sometimes it was very hard for me to listen and not react. With time I developed an empathy toward the people I interviewed. I did not always agree with them, but I could understand them better. I even got used to the way they used various words. At first the word *schwarze*[1] sounded terrible to me, and I was certain that those who used it had a negative attitude toward the blacks. With time I could gather from the way they said it what it really meant to them. Most people did not mean anything derogatory by using *schwarze*; it was simply a descriptive term. The few who used it in a negative sense pronounced it in a different way.

The fact that I understood a little Yiddish was also a great advantage. I discovered this one morning when I was sitting in the Jewish Philanthropies' drop-in center. An elderly man said something in Yiddish and, without thinking, I reacted in the same language. This caused general admiration: I was accepted by the elderly and was even offered bagels with cream cheese. Most of them spoke English fluently, but Yiddish was their in-group language. It was not important that my Yiddish was broken; the fact that the old people realized that I understood the language helped me a great deal while interviewing them. Although we always talked in English, they would use Yiddish words without even noticing it.

The Sample

It is very difficult to carry out a study in a changing neighborhood since people are constantly moving out. Doing fieldwork in such an area is, in a way, running against time. One never knows if those one intends to interview are still living in the neighborhood.

When I began the study I intended to interview 100 Jewish people in Mattapan. Although nobody was able to supply a list of the Jewish residents of the area, I picked out all the names in the 1972 voting registration lists which sounded Jewish to me. Although this was by no means an accurate list, it was the only way to identify the Jewish people.

After the first few days in the field, I realized that my list of Jewish names was not too reliable. Many people who were supposed to live in the area were no longer there. On my first day I visited an apartment building which presumably had twelve Jewish families—but had none. The only one on my list, a person named Fisher, who turned out to be non-Jewish, explained to me that when the Jewish owner sold the building to a black, all of the elderly Jewish women left. In some cases names were ambiguous; and there were a few exceptions, such as a black couple named Blum. As demonstrated above, my accuracy in identifying Jewish residents by their names proved fallible on several occasions.

This, however, was not my major problem. More serious was the fact that I never knew whether I would find the person I was looking for. In the old apartment buildings, entrances were often dark, and it was hard to find out who was living there. Very often no names appeared on the doors, especially in single-family houses. From my experience in the area I learned that when a big, new car was parked in front of a house, the residents were usually black. Sometimes when I rang a bell, a black woman would answer and say, "Mrs. Gittelman left two weeks ago." In one house the *Mezuza*[2] was left on the door. Although it was frustrating to walk around with a list and find out that many people were no longer there, the discrepancy between my information and what I found was a good indicator of the degree of change in different streets in Mattapan.

It was clear that in a neighborhood where people were constantly moving out it would be impossible to pick out a random sample of 100 Jewish people. Eighty-five of the 250 people to whom I sent my letter left Mattapan before the study began. In some cases I was able to check the addresses before sending out the letters. Thus the actual number of absent people was much higher.

Another factor which made it difficult to draw a sample was the relatively high rate of refusals. Of the 250 people, 85 left before the study began; 36 were not Jewish or were not at home; 37 refused to answer; and 92 were interviewed (8 people were interviewed before the letters were sent out). In spite of the impossible task of drawing a systematic sample, I intended to choose the interviewees according to the three following criteria:

1. Age. As already indicated, the majority of the remaining Mattapan Jews were elderly. Many changes occur when people become older. The interaction between limitations caused by age and the problems of the changing neighborhood makes situations even more difficult for those people. Although there were hardly any young Jewish adults in Mattapan, it seemed important to compare the older people with those younger. Since the lists I had specified only those who were over sixty years old and did not give any further distinction of age, I tried to pick a sample of people sixty years and older and those who were younger.

2. Type of ownership. Many studies of changing neighborhoods have dealt with the impact of ownership on racial transition. It seemed therefore important to compare owners with renters. Type of ownership was taken into consideration while choosing the sample. (The main problem was that in the two-family houses there was no way to know in advance whether the person owned the house or was a tenant.)

3. *Georgraphical location*. The remaining Mattapan Jews were scattered in different sections of the area. Since the racial change did not occur in all sections simultaneously, at the time of this study some Jews lived on streets which were in the process of change while others lived on streets which were almost all black. A few Jews lived on streets which had not yet changed. Also, whereas most Jews lived in the Jewish area of Mattapan, some lived in the predominantly non-Jewish section. People living in different sections of Mattapan were represented in the study.

Because the area was changing constantly, even while the study was being conducted, the sample was much less systematic than I had originally intended. Yet all categories mentioned above were included.

Description of the Sample

1. *Age*.

TABLE 9
The People Interviewed, by Age

Age in Years	Number of People Interviewed
70 and over	33
60-69	30
50-59	22
40-49	10
30-39	2
29 and less	3
	Total 100

The age composition of the Jewish population was of course reflected in the sample, with 63% of the people interviewed sixty years or older. (Only the age of the head of the family or his wife was taken into account.)

2. *Family size*. As already indicated, the Jewish families of Mattapan were small. This was true also for the people interviewed—the median size of a family was 2.1 persons. The majority of the families interviewed (fifty-one) consisted of two persons. Of the rest, seventeen families consisted of three persons, twelve families consisted of four persons, and nineteen were single-person households. In twenty-seven cases I interviewed both husband and wife, and in eight cases teenage or adult children participated in the interview.

3. *Occupation*.

TABLE 10
Family Heads by Occupation

Occupation	Number of Family Heads in that Occupation
Professional and Technical	6
Managers and Proprietors	8
Sales and Clerical	18
Blue Collar	29
Unemployed	3
Retired	36
Total	100

Over one-third of the people interviewed were retired at that time. This is not surprising taking into account the older age of the population. Almost one-half of those who were still in the labor force were blue-collar workers, mostly craftsmen and taxi cab drivers, while a few were laborers and service workers. The six professionals consisted of two teachers, a social worker, two accountants, and one IBM technician. Six of the eight managers and proprietors were self-employed store owners.

4. *Ownership*. Forty-seven of the people interviewed were home owners and fifty-three were renters. Although there was no

way to find out the proportion of Jewish owners and renters, it seems that owners were somewhat over-represented in the sample. This was unavoidable since many renters were concentrated in the fairly new housing complexes, and I tried to select a more or less dispersed sample.

5. *Location*. Although I tried to choose the sample from different sections of Mattapan, it was determined by the actual location of the Jews. There were very few Jews living in the predominantly black area at that time. Twenty of the people interviewed lived in the more or less all-black area, eight of them inside the "red line." Twenty-four people lived in the predominantly non-Jewish section on the southern edge of Mattapan. In addition, seventeen of those interviewed lived in apartment buildings populated mainly by Jews but which were located close to the non-Jewish section. The remaining thirty-nine people were dispersed in Jewish or somewhat mixed sections. Since the neighborhood is constantly changing, however, this area is becoming more and more black, and it is difficult to draw a line between the various sections of Mattapan.

NOTES

1 The Yiddish translation of the word "black." It is an impersonal term which often has a negative connotation.

2 A piece of parchment inscribed on one side with texts from the Bible; it is rolled, put into a case, and attached to the door post of the house.

CHAPTER FOUR

Residential History

In this chapter we will deal with the residential mobility patterns of the Mattapan Jews and discuss their reasons for choosing their present homes. We will examine in some detail their social network and their neighborly relation. Finally, we will describe their housing conditions.

Residential Mobility

The residential history of the Mattapan Jews represents to some extent the history of the Jewish community in Boston. About half of the people interviewed were born in this country, and some, among the younger ones, are already third generation. Most of those who were born abroad came to the United States around the time of World War I or in the early 1920's and have lived here for fifty years. Only a few people arrived in this country after World War II.

Many of the older people who were born in Boston came originally from the West End. They began moving gradually into Roxbury and Dorchester and from there into Mattapan. Another path of residential mobility seemed to be from Chelsea (a city on the northern edge of Boston), which had at that time a large Jewish population, and from there via Roxbury and Dorchester to Mattapan.

Those who came from abroad, and the younger native Americans, started out in Roxbury and moved southward from there. Mattapan seemed to be the final destination in this residential mobility pattern. A few younger people were born in the northern part of Mattapan, and one claimed to be "a Mattapan girl." They moved about in the area itself. According to people's recollections, Mattapan was once a high-status area in which many rich Jews lived.

Although most people stayed in the same geographical area for most of their lives, it seems that many moved from one apartment to another quite frequently. Usually they only moved a short distance. Those who in the past owned houses in Roxbury or Dorchester seemed to be less mobile than the rest, and some even lived in their previous homes for thirty or forty years. Twenty-six people had previously lived in other apartments in Mattapan itself and had moved from there to their present place of residence.

A few people, mainly owners, had been living in their present homes for quite a long time—eleven to twenty years or more. Most people, however, had moved to their present address more recently; the median length of residence for the interviewees was seven years. (According to the 1970 census, 52% of the White population moved to its present location after 1965.) As one would expect, owners were more stable than renters: the median length of residence for owners was twelve years compared to four years for renters. Only a few renters had lived in their present apartments for more than eight years. The fact that half of the renters and a few owners moved into their present apartments in the last four years is interesting, as the area had already begun to change at that time. As other studies have indicated, it seems that renters are more willing to move into an already changing neighborhood than owners. (Wolf and Lebeaux, 1969.)

People moved out of their apartments or houses for various reasons. Some lived in apartments and wanted to have houses of their own. For others, their apartments were too small and they needed more space. These seem to be the most common reasons for residential mobility. (Rossi, 1955.) Older people, on the other hand, felt that they did not need a large apartment or house anymore. "We had ten rooms, my sons got married and moved out and it was too big for us. Also, it was too much work for me." For elderly people a house can become a burden, especially if one has to shovel the snow in the winter. Most of them moved to smaller apartments where everything is maintained for them. The death of a husband was also listed as a reason to sell a house. "My husband died and I couldn't stand the house anymore." A few renters left their apartments because they did not get along with their landlords or because the latter sold the building.

Many of those who changed their residence in the last ten years moved out of Roxbury or Dorchester or even out of the northern part of Mattapan because blacks moved into the area. "All the *schmutzniks* [dirt] came and it was impossible to live there with children." "The blacks started moving in and it became very bad—I don't want to describe their parties. Many women lived there without their husbands, and men came to visit them and knocked on our door. We couldn't sleep at night so we decided to move." Others were worried about the crime. "Everytime I left the apartment I used to carry the television and other things to the basement because the apartments above and below mine were robbed. Once I was held up by six black youngsters during the day. They didn't take much and nothing happened to me, but after that I decided to move." A few people recalled that they "saw the writing on the wall" and moved before it was too late. More often, however, people claimed that they were "practically the only white people on the street." In retrospect, it seems that almost everyone was the only white person left on his street. Some who lived close to the junior high school in Mattapan moved because they were afraid of the black teenagers. "They threw rocks into my windows, my apartment was robbed three times, I couldn't walk on the street even during the day." (According to the 1970 census, the area around the school was the first to change in Mattapan.)

Home owners realized that they could not find white tenants in a changing neighborhood. Some rented to blacks, but others preferred to sell. "The *schwarze* [blacks] came in and I was afraid I'd have to rent to them. No white people came into the area anymore, so I sold the house and moved." Others did not want black tenants for other reasons—"You cannot rely on them with the rent, you have to run after them till they pay." These owners picked their tenants on a highly selective basis, and like the local resident owners Krohn studied in Montreal (Krohn and Tilly, 1969), would not take a tenant who did not seem right to them.

The fact that many people had lived in a changing neighborhood in the past seems to have had an impact on their present behavior.

Why Did They Choose Their Present Homes?

The Housing Aspect

Most people chose their place of residence for the same reasons they moved out of their previous homes or apartments. Many decided to move because they wanted a better home. Space and especially ownership were the main considerations. In this respect they do not differ from other Americans who are moving to the suburbs (Gans, 1967). For most home owners it was the first time in their lives that they had owned a house. "That was the first time since we got married that we owned a house." "We lived in a six-family house, we wanted a house of our own, we saw it and we liked it." "We wanted a house for our children."

Space was also an important consideration for the owners as well as the renters. "It is a good apartment, we have two floors with seven rooms. We have a porch and a garage." Also, people paid attention to the condition of the building—the fact that Mattapan has had a fairly new housing stock was regarded as an advantage. "We saw it and liked the place, the apartments were new and nice." "I wanted to buy a fairly new house and that one isn't too old."

Above all, the question of price seemed to be important. "We were looking for a house which wasn't too expensive." "That house was what we could afford, so we bought it." The combination of good housing at a relatively inexpensive price was no doubt an important factor in the decision-making process. "My husband is a proud man, he won't buy his wife an old house. He couldn't afford to buy a ranch house in Brookline or Newton, so he bought a brand new ranch house here." The consideration of price was taken into account by renters also, but to a lesser extent. "In Brookline, the rent for an apartment like this is $250" (they paid $200). The question of price had in some cases an effect on the kind of house the people were looking for. "We couldn't afford a one-family house, so we thought we'd buy a two-family and the tenant will help us pay for the house."

In most cases owners found their houses through formal channels. "We were reading the builder's ad in the paper; we came to look at it and liked it." Although many renters found their apartments in the same way, some learned about vacancies from friends or relatives. A few older people who had moved into the new apartment buildings in the last few years claimed that their children urged them to leave their former homes and had found their present apartments for them. Some did not have time to look for a new place. "I was so anxious to leave that I took the first apartment I saw."

The Locational Aspect

We have already seen that one of the considerations for choosing a house or apartment in Mattapan was that housing in this area was cheaper than in other neighborhoods. However, many people chose the area because of its own advantages, such as the fact that it is in the city and has many of the facilities of an urban area. "This was the best neighborhood one could find. It's close to everywhere, good transportation, good shopping area." "In two mintues you are near everything." "It's very handy here, close to the MBTA and to the stores; I don't drive and have to be close to everything."

The convenient location is very important for people working in the city. "My husband has a laundry in Roxbury and we couldn't move too far away." "If you don't have a car, you have to live in the city, you cannot go to places like Randolph [a suburban town about eight miles south of Boston]." The good shopping facilities are regarded as an additional advantage. "I wouldn't like to live in the suburbs; I like to live in a place where I can walk to the shopping area."

Besides being an urban neighborhood, Mattapan has many of the advantages of a suburban area. There are small houses with a good deal of open space and even woods. "It's very nice and quite like in the country." "It looked like a nice neighborhood, nice new houses with porches to sit on in the summer, a lot of green." "It's close to the woods and to the Blue Mountains, the air is good, it's cooler here than in the city." In other words, the combination of the semisuburban area inside the city with good transportation and a large shopping center seemed to attract many Jews to Mattapan. They are aware of the fact that the area is one of the few neighborhoods in Boston which has the advantages of a city and a suburb.

Some mentioned the social characteristics of the area, liking the fact that it was different from the suburbs. "People who lived here were lower middle-class, working people. People who worked hard and sent their kids to college. They wanted to live here—they didn't want to move to the suburbs and keep up with everybody. Here they didn't need to send their kids to nursery school and buy new furniture. They had good transportation and didn't need a second car." Or, somebody else commented on the social status of the neighborhood. "We were all in the same boat, not rich but quite middle class—a policeman, a salesman, my husband was an engineer."

The Importance of Living in a Jewish Neighborhood

For most people the fact that Mattapan was a Jewish neighborhood was a very important consideration in their choice of residence. Most of these people had lived in Jewish neighborhoods all their lives, and it seemed to most the natural thing to do. Many of them reacted angrily when I asked them whether it was important for them to live in a Jewish area; they could not understand how one could question it. "Naturally, I am a Jew." Some explained that "I hardly knew any gentile people; I lived among Jews all my life, I used to enjoy it. When I moved to this apartment I was glad that it was a building with all Jewish families." "We grew up in a Jewish area, we liked our little ghetto. I don't mind it a little bit mixed, but still I like to be among my own kind."

Basically, most people had a similar reaction—they felt more comfortable among their own kind. "I want to live in a Jewish area, you feel more *himish* [at home] there." "It's important to live with Jews because you want to live with people like yourself. When my wife goes shopping she will not chat with a gentile, she wants to do it with her own kind." "I like to live in a Jewish neighborhood, I feel more comfortable among my own people. I don't want to live where I am not wanted." And one woman simply said, "I don't want to hear anybody say 'dirty Jew' to me."

Perhaps the best summary of this attitude was "There are good Jews and bad Jews, but they are your own kind. You can talk with them." It is no wonder that many of these people chose their residences because they knew they were in a Jewish area. "I knew that many Jews were living in this building, although I didn't know them."

Only a very few people mentioned the importance of being close to Jewish institutions, such as a synagogue, a kosher butcher, or even a Jewish newspaper, as a reason for living in a Jewish area. It may well be, however, that many were taking these facilities for granted.

Some of the people I interviewed were confronted with a choice such as this: "Before we bought this house I wanted to buy a lot in Quincy [an old city on the southern border of Boston]. It was before Christmas and we drove by. When my wife saw all of the Christmas trees she didn't want to live there, there were no Jews there. So we decided to buy this house." One woman recalled choosing the area in spite of her past experience with blacks and the suspicion that the neighborhood was going to change. "I gave the area five years, but I wanted to live in a Jewish neighborhood. I feel more comfortable among Jews. I don't have to pretend. Where could I go? In South Boston they won't let any blacks in, but I didn't want to live among *goyim* [gentiles]."

The importance of living in a Jewish area varied for people at different stages of life. It seems that for elderly people, on the one hand, and for parents with children on the other, their family composition was a major consideration in their decision. With the elderly, it was because they had lived in a Jewish area all their lives. As for parents with children, they wanted their children to associate with other Jewish children. "I have three daughters and if God is good to me they'll marry a Jew." It seems clear that for people without small children this was less important. "My children were already in high school and it wasn't important to live on a Jewish street." On the other hand, some of those living in the predominantly non-Jewish section of Mattapan chose to do so deliberately because "we wanted to give our children an opportunity to live in a mixed area."

Although those living in the non-Jewish section were obviously a minority, their reasons for choosing this area are worth mentioning. Only a few moved there because the houses were older and therefore less expensive than in the Jewish area. Most, however, claimed to have chosen a non-Jewish street deliberately. "We were the only Jews on the street. I didn't want to live in a ghetto, I wanted my children to know that there are other children too." "I wouldn't want to live in a Jewish neighborhood. I want my privacy and you can't have it in a Jewish area. People think that because they are your own kind they can always come to your house."

In contrast to most Mattapan Jews, those living in the mixed area by choice had grown up in a non-Jewish neighborhood. "I wanted to live in a mixed neighborhood. I was used to it. We always had *goyim* neighbors." However, these Jews were not always warmly greeted by their gentile neighbors. "We heard later that the neighbors weren't happy that a Jew moved in, but they were nice to us. . . ." Some recalled that their neighbors used to say that the area had started to change twenty years ago when the first Jew moved in. So, although these people had chosen to live in a non-Jewish area, they admitted being happy when a second Jewish family moved onto their street. They also liked the fact that the Jewish area was not too far away. "On the other hand, it was close enough to the Jewish area and I used to shop in the Jewish stores. I wouldn't like to live far away from a Jewish area."

Social Network

Mattapan was part of the larger Jewish community of Boston, which included Roxbury and Dorchester. Although many Mattapan Jews had friends and relatives in this larger community, very often those people did not live in their immediate vicinity. It seems that about one-fourth of the people interviewed had relatives in Mattapan proper.

The existence of relatives and friends in the immediate vicinity did not seem to be an important consideration in choosing the present place of residence. Very few claimed they moved because they had family or social ties in their immediate vicinity. However, there were some exceptions to this, such as one elderly woman who moved to her present apartment because her daughter lived on the same street; or another woman who moved to a new apartment building because her two sisters already lived in the same complex. One woman explained that they did not buy a house in a southern suburb because her parents still lived in Dorchester and she did not want to live too far from them.

Most people apparently did not know anybody on their street or block. However, most knew that the street or apartment building was inhabited by Jews, and that was the important factor. "You want to live with your own kind, although I didn't have anything to do with my neighbors."

In most cases—at least that is the way it seems now— Mattapan Jews had only limited contact with their neighbors. "We are not the type to mingle with neighbors, we keep to ourselves. I don't even know who is living in this building, I only know the people on my floor, but we don't visit them and they don't visit us." "I don't mix with neighbors, we say 'Hi' and that's it. I am not a *yente* [gossip]." Most people recalled that they were friendly with their neighbors, but the relationship seemed to be superficial. "We were friendly but no more than that; we said 'Hello' on the street." Of course, some people did chat with their neighbors on the street.

The friendly relations with neighbors in many cases meant such social exchanges as sending Christmas cards or Jewish New Year cards. Many people made the clear distinction that "neighbors were neighbors and friends were friends," or that "our real friends do not live here." (When people used the word "here," they meant in their close vicinity, that is, in their street or block group. Those who had friends in the other end of Mattapan did not consider them neighbors.) Because of this sort of superficial relationship with neighbors, it seems that for some people it did not really make any difference whether their neighbors were gentiles or Jews. "I didn't mind living in a non-Jewish street because all of my friends are Jewish and they don't live here."

There were, of course, exceptions to this kind of neighborly relationship. Some kept their friendship with neighbors on a rather formal basis. "I am friendly with one neighbor, but usually we don't go in until we are invited." A few reported that they had a "bagel club" on the street, but, "We didn't visit in the houses, we always met in the yards. We weren't the type of *yentes* [gossipers] to go into other people's homes."

In a few cases people reported that they used to visit their neighbors. "When I moved in, I knew one girl on the street, but with time I had many friends here. I knew I could always drop in for coffee." Or an elderly woman said: "People are very friendly in this building, most are widows like myself. We visit each other and play bingo once a week. If we need something, we go and borrow; it's really a good feeling." Another elderly woman who lived in a building which once consisted of ten Jewish families and then only had two lamented that "It was like one big family." These examples are exceptions, for most people did not have this kind of informal relationship with their neighbors, "Not like in the old days when neighbors used to come in."

Some explanations for the lack of social relations were given by the people themselves. Age and life cycle stage were mentioned. "Maybe when you move to an area when you have young children you socialize with neighbors." Or, "You make friends when you are young, but not at my age." It seems that those few people who apparently had closer relations with neighbors moved into their present homes when they had young children and had lived there for quite a long time. Although one could expect that old people would become close friends with their neighbors, in most cases it was not so. Another explanation for the lack of close relations was that "I didn't have much contact with the neighbors because I have always been working."

In retrospect, it is difficult to judge whether this kind of loose social network was really typical of the Jewish community of Mattapan. From remarks, however, it seems that "This neighborhood isn't as cohesive as it was years ago" (mentioned by a seventy-year-old man who had lived in Mattapan for more than fifty years). Another man noticed that "It isn't like the North End. I once drove by and saw people on the street cooking barbeque for each other. Here it isn't like this, it wasn't that kind of community." Some people even complained about their previous neighbors. "It wasn't a friendly neighborhood, people here were very cold. Sometimes my next door neighbor didn't even say hello."

The fact that most people were just friendly but not close to their neighbors did not seem to bother them. What was important for the Mattapan Jews was the fact that they knew their neighbors, or even as one man put it, "We knew their faces but we didn't know them." They recognized their neighbors and that was the main thing. One woman summarized this attitude: "We were friendly but not more, we just said hello on the street. The thing was we knew everybody here." Or, as another person said, "It was nice to walk on the street and to know people. We knew we belonged here, although I never had real friends in this area."

Many community studies emphasize the role of the social network in creating neighborhood cohesiveness. (Young and Willmott, 1957; Fried, 1963.) Suttles argues that sentimental attachment to neighbors is not the only kind of residential cohesion:

> From the point of view of the local resident, the most elemental grouping of his coresidence is usually a network of acquaintances who have been selected primarily because they are known from shared conditions of residence and the common usage of local facilities. They are acquaintances who are recog-

nized on face to face relations or encounters. (Suttles, 1972, p. 55.)

This description seems to fit the type of neighborly relations which most Mattapan Jews used to have.

The fact that most people did not have close social relations with their neighbors does not mean that they were isolated. Most of them had friends either in different parts of Mattapan or in other areas. It seems that for most people it did not matter whether their friends lived in their close vicinity or farther away because "with the car, it's no problem." Many women belonged to "clubs" and met their friends once a week to play cards. These were not block clubs because most people did not live on the same block. And since they had to drive even if their friends only lived in another area of Mattapan, it did not actually make a difference whether those friends lived in Mattapan or in Randolph or in Brookline or Newton.

Housing Conditions

As we have already noticed, most of the Jewish people who still resided in Mattapan lived in housing which was in good condition. Only a few lived in old apartment buildings such as three-deckers or six-family houses. Most lived in single- or two-family houses or in fairly new apartment buildings. Twenty-seven of the forty-seven owners lived in houses which had been built in the last sixteen to twenty years. Nine of them were two-family houses, most commonly a two-story house in which a tenant lived upstairs or downstairs. Most of the owners of the fairly new houses lived in single ranch houses. The typical house consisted of six rooms and a spacious basement.

Twenty owners lived in older houses, many of them in the predominantly non-Jewish section. Although the houses were older, they were in good condition, and often people invested money and renovated them. These were more frequently (thirteen) two-family rather than single houses. Unlike the new houses, the number of rooms varied from one house to another, from four to eight rooms, while most houses consisted of five to six rooms. Those owners who had lived in their house for twenty years or more had finished paying their mortgages. The majority were still paying for their houses, with the monthly payments ranging from $140 up to $200 in a few cases.

The renters can be divided into three groups according to their housing conditions. One small group lived in the three-deckers or six-family apartment buildings. These buildings were usually in the northern part of Mattapan, and many of them were run down and in poor condition. In most cases the landlord was absent. Another group of tenants lived in the two-family houses, some in the new ones, but more frequently in the older houses, most of which were in good condition. Almost half of the tenants lived in new apartment buildings, most of them built during the last ten years. Seventeen of the renters lived in two big housing complexes in the southern part of Mattapan, and another eight were scattered in new apartment buildings throughout the area. One of the apartment complexes had about 350 units and was quite luxurious. It had a swimming pool, and the apartments were equipped with air conditioning, dishwashers, and wall-to-wall carpeting. The new buildings consisted of one- and two-bedroom apartments with the rents ranging from about $180 to $235.

Tenants in the old apartment buildings or in the two-family houses paid less rent, although these apartments were more spacious in most cases. The rents ranged from less than $100 for a three-room apartment in a three-decker house to about $180 for a seven-room apartment.

It is interesting to note that a few of the renters who were owners in the past had moved out of their previous houses in the last few years because of the blacks and because it seemed too risky to them to buy a house in this area. "When I moved here I gave the area five years, but I didn't care. It isn't my property and I am not going to lose money."

Owner-Tenant Relations

Twenty-two of the forty-seven owners had tenants. They usually lived in two-family houses with a tenant upstairs or downstairs who "helps us pay the rent." Except for three cases in which the tenants were relatives, the tenants were strangers. Some people bought the house "with" the tenant, that is, the tenant was already living there when they moved in. Among the nineteen owners who had tenants who were not relatives, thirteen had Jewish tenants and six had non-Jewish ones. None of the Jewish owners had a black tenant. It seems that most Jewish owners were selective about their tenants' ethnic backgrounds. Many claimed, however, that they had had gentile tenants in the past and that it did not make any difference. Most owners had had the same tenant for a number of years, some for ten years and even more. The Jewish tenants seemed to have been there longer than the gentile tenants.

Some owners complained about their tenants, one man even saying, "We have very bad tenants upstairs, we never had tenants like this. They are Jewish but I'll tell you *schwarze* are better." In most cases, however, the relations with the tenants seemed to be good. Social contact, however, was restricted. "We are friendly but not too friendly. They are nice, they don't bother us and we don't bother them." Or a woman remarked about her very stable tenants, "I have been up maybe three times in fifteen years."

Although most owners had a tenant to "help them pay the rent," they were more concerned with a good tenant than with making money. "They are just two people and we don't want them to leave because they don't make noise. We didn't raise their rent." "We do not raise her rent because we don't want her to leave and a colored come in." In this respect the Mattapan owners resembled the local resident owners Krohn described in

Montreal who were "more concerned with their property as residence, and set economics into second place." (Krohn and Tilly, 1969, p. 13.) One man even admitted, "I'll feel bad for my tenants to sell the house to blacks."

This noneconomic attitude was not exclusively shared by the resident owners. Krohn distinguishes between the local owner who is selective about his tenants, wants to keep his property, and therefore will not raise the rent, and the absentee landlord who wants to make a quick profit and does not care who his tenants are. From the stories of the Mattapan tenants, it seems that the absentee landlords did not always fit Krohn's typology: "Last time the neighbor upstairs moved out the landlady didn't advertise in the paper. She knows that only a black family will come in, and that will be the end of her property because the whites will move out. The apartment was empty for three months until a white person took it!"

All of the renters who lived in the new apartment buildings had absentee landlords and dealt with the management. Of the other twenty-eight renters, sixteen had resident owners. These were mainly the two-family houses where the owner lived in the house. The tenants whose landlords were absent lived in the older three-deckers or six-family houses in most cases. Some of them complained that their landlord did not take care of the house. (In this respect the absentee landlord did fit Krohn's typology.) In contrast to the owners who had predominantly Jewish tenants, only five of the sixteen tenants living with the owner in the same building had Jewish landlords. It seems that the Jewish tenants were less selective about the ethnic background of their landlords than the Jewish owners were about their tenants.

Although most renters had lived in their present homes for a shorter period than the owners, some of them had lived in the same place quite a long time, even staying in the house when the original owner sold it. In this way, three Jewish families living in two-family houses had black landlords living in the same house with them. All three seemed to be very satisfied with their black landlords. "They keep the house better than the Italian who owned it before; they don't bother us; it's like having our own house." "The first thing our black landlady did was to put new locks all over the house and a fence."

CHAPTER FIVE

Living in a Changing Neighborhood

In this chapter we will describe the process of change from the point of view of those who, remaining in the area, lived through this change. We will first discuss how the Mattapan Jews felt in realizing that their neighborhood was changing and what the main indicators of change were from their point of view. We will then examine the impact of these changes on their own way of life and see how they coped with the new situation. We will try to relate behavioral differences to various factors such as specific location inside Mattapan and life cycle stage. We will also deal with the problem of crime and fear. We will discuss social relations in a changing neighborhood, and finally, we will try to understand why the Mattapan Jews remained in the area.

In What Way Has the Neighborhood Changed?

One of the most common reactions of the Mattapan Jews to their changing neighborhood was one of surprise. In spite of the fact that the area began changing about five years before this study was done and that some people had lived in a changing neighborhood before, most were caught by surprise at the fact that their immediate area or street was changing. "It came so fast; they are all over." "We never thought it would come so fast." "It all came so quickly; it hits you all of a sudden." Although some people, as we have seen, claimed they predicted the area was going to change, for most the change came as something of a shock. "We didn't think they'd come to the ranch houses." Even those who claim they expected blacks to move toward Mattapan, did not expect it would change so rapidly. "We gave the area ten years and it took less than five."

The change was of course that whites, in most cases Jews, were moving out of the area and blacks were moving in. Although most people could not exactly remember how and when it started, we can get a fairly clear idea of how the neighborhood changed. According to what most people recall, their residential area started changing within two or three years before I started this study. There were, of course, differences in the various sections of Mattapan. A few streets on the border of the area had not yet changed, that is, blacks had not moved there. Other streets had changed only within a year prior to this study. Despite these differences, most people referred to the last two or three years when speaking of the change (the exceptions were, of course, those who lived on streets with no blacks).

Another significant point is that when people talked about changes in their area, they referred to a very small territorial unit, to a block group of a few houses. "This part of the street changed in the last two years; it's 75% black. I don't know what's on the other side across Messinger Street." Thus, people realized that *their* neighborhood was changing only when the changes occurred close to their homes.

The First Owner Who Sold to Blacks

How did their neighborhood start to change? Most emphasized that people were always buying and selling. There are only a very few streets where people have not moved out in the last years. Thus, the Mattapan Jews distinguished between what they call sales for "legitimate reasons" and those of panic and fear. The legitimate reasons were many. In some cases people needed more space or they "outgrew their houses." Others moved because a husband or wife died and they did not need so much space and could not take care of the house.

So, the problem in their eyes was not why people sold, but rather why they sold to blacks. Although many admitted that people sold for various reasons which had nothing to do with the neighborhood, many blamed the first who sold to blacks as the ones who caused the racial change in their area. "The first one who sold didn't get along with the neighbors and he sold to blacks to show them. He did not care." Those who accuse the first who sold deliberately claim, of course, that at that time it was still possible to sell to white people. Thus, they regard those who did not get along with neighbors responsible for the racial change. This same story was repeated by various people on different streets.

Few people admitted that at a certain point even the first seller could not sell to whites anymore. "It started here about two years ago. The first one who sold was an old Jewish lady. First she sold to white people but they couldn't find the money; so she got impatient and sold to blacks." Some claim that the first who sold to blacks "couldn't resist making money." "The first Jew who sold his house on Woodhaven Street sold it for $45,000. He made a lot of money. You see, Jews are a little bit greedy; I mean the first ones who sold. They didn't care about their neighbors; they didn't care if the area got black; they didn't care about leaving a good name."

The Chain Reaction

Whether the first owner who sold to blacks did it deliberately or not, the result seems to be the same—a chain reaction of panic selling. "In a week three other families were selling. Before you knew, everybody was selling. Suddenly I saw people moving out and blacks moving in." Thus, when the first wave of change hit the street, people just moved out. "They didn't tell anybody. The next door neighbor lived here for nine years and one morning we saw the truck! She didn't even come to say good-bye." "The next thing you saw was people starting to move out. It was sickening to see it. They wouldn't say anything; you'd just see the truck coming and people moving. Maybe they felt guilty. I don't know."

The way people left the area of course caused a lot of rumors and suspicion among neighbors. Neighbors claiming they were not selling moved out a few days later. Others, putting a sign "mine not for sale" on their window, sold in spite of it. A woman living on a street which had begun to change only a few months before said, "It's like a detective game; each month we are guessing who is going to sell." Some people learned of their neighbors' intention to sell when they saw blacks coming to the house, and "It's obvious they are not coming to visit." The reaction of the remaining Jews to their former neighbors seems understandable. "They did it without telling anybody. I don't mind the fact that they sold; everybody is entitled to do with his house whatever he wants. I resent the way they did it." Later, after the first wave of panic selling was over, people no longer tried to hide the fact that they were moving, and one could see many "for sale" signs on certain streets.

People tried to explain the chain reaction caused by the first black moving onto the street. The general view was that "they were panicky." Some were simply afraid of blacks, others were worried that the longer they waited, the more the value of their property would drop because "As more blacks move onto the street, you lose more money." The loss of money is relative; people realized that those who sold got a higher price for their houses than the price they paid when they bought them. However, most noticed that if the same houses had been in another area, the owners would have gotten more for them—that prices went up everywhere but in Mattapan. Also, some people invested in their houses, and it was hard to get the investment back.

Crime was another reason why people moved out. "My neighbor across the street was beaten up in front of his house. So his wife said, 'Why should we wait,' and they moved out." Some mentioned the schools as a reason for parents with school-age children to move out. However, that reason seemed to have little to do with the changes in the immediate vicinity and more with the area in general.

The overall result of the rapid change was that "in a very short period everyone I knew on the street was gone." "Now the whole street has changed, we do not feel it's our community any more." And, therefore, some of the people felt like "the last of the Mohicans." People living in rented apartments also felt the change. "When we first moved here two years ago there were nine Jewish families in the building; now there is only one other Jewish family here."

Perhaps what is most impressive about this process of change, according to people's recollections, was how fast it all happened. The general feeling was that it "catches on like a disease" or that the blacks entered their street "like ants," "like fire," or "like mushrooms after the rain." "They come like a tide, first it's a trickle and then it's a stream; you cannot stop it."

Indicators of a Changing Neighborhood

For some people the fact that blacks were moving into the area was a sign that Mattapan was not as good a neighborhood as it used to be. A woman living in one of the apartment complexes remarked: "In the last two years I think this place went down. Colored people started moving into the area. I don't say they shouldn't come, they must live somewhere, but the place isn't as good as it used to be. People get scared from all the stories they hear." The moment blacks moved into the apartment complexes, there were vacancies. "When we moved here a year and a half ago, you had to wait on the waiting list to get in. Now there are vacancies and they are coming in." That indicated to the people that the place was not as desirable as it once was; that it was probably "going down." Therefore, the rents they paid for their apartments, and which were regarded as reasonable in the past, were "Too high for an area with a bad name like Mattapan." A few people reported that the reason some of their neighbors left was the rents they had to pay. Although it seems true, as some studies claim, that people are more ready to rent than buy in a changing neighborhood (Wolf and Lebeaux, 1969), it also seems that people expect other benefits, such as lower rents for staying in the area.

Another indication that the area was "going down" is that apartment buildings changed hands frequently. One woman noticed that from the time she moved into the building seven years before this study was made, it had already had four owners! The frequent change of ownership sometimes resulted, at least in the eyes of the people, in bad maintainence.

What Happened after the First Wave of Change Was Over?

First, people claimed, "all houses around here are for sale," and many had the feeling that "everybody is moving." As a result more and more blacks moved into the area. "Now if you see a white person walking on the street, it's strange because all are blacks. I'm almost the only white person here." The change is visible, and people admitted that "at the beginning it was strange to see so many colored people."

Two situations seemed hard for people to get used to. First

was the fact that they suddenly saw black people on their streets. "When the first one moved in we felt somewhat uncomfortable— suddenly to look out of the window and see black faces. We weren't used to it." Second, it was difficult for the people to adjust to the change itself. "At first it was frightening to see the area changing, but you get used to it."

The change was not only that now black people lived on "their" street, but also that the moment blacks moved into the area, one saw more and more blacks around. "The moment colored people live here, a lot of colored just walk around. [Therefore] you see only colored people when you look out of the window." Or another woman made the following remark: "After the first family moves in, you suddenly see them driving on the streets."

Many people lamented the "beautiful area" which was gone. It was assumed by most of them that the area was "going down." Most people noticed physical changes despite the fact that most agreed the black homeowners took care of their property and kept their houses in good condition. "There is a lot of rubbish around. You can see when they are coming, there is a lot of garbage." As a result streets were not as clean as they used to be. Also, city services deteriorated. "Each winter they'd come and plow the snow; this winter we had to call them several times after each snow storm." (There is no way to check the extent to which this claim is based on reality.) A few people admitted that no such changes occurred on the streets. "It was a beautiful area, I still think it's a very nice area. Now it changed, but I mean you don't see it from the outside that it changed." Of course, not all of Mattapan changed at once, and differences occur from one street to the next. Some streets have changed almost completely; some are in the process of change; and a few have not yet changed. Also, as mentioned earlier, not all the streets in Mattapan look alike. In general one can say that whereas most streets in the southern part are clean, some streets in the northern part look dirty and neglected.

Changes in the Commercial Area

The immediate vicinity or block group is only one territorial entity to which people referred. "I love my house and that's a nice street, but you don't only live on the street, you live in an area." The block group is an area too small to carry out daily activities such as shopping (Suttles, 1972). People used a much broader territory and noticed, of course, the changes in the commercial area.

The commercial area of Mattapan consists of two main parts, the shopping area along Blue Hill Avenue and Mattapan Square. Blue Hill Avenue looks depressing, and it is obvious to the Mattapan Jews that a once-large shopping area is gone. To most of them this loss indicates more than anything else the changes in the area. All the people I interviewed, regardless of the street they lived on, referred to the changes on the Avenue, and to the fact that it looked "terrible." "Did you see Blue Hill Avenue? It was a beautiful shopping area; now all the stores are boarded." "All the stores are burned down and it looks like a plywood city." Another indication that the area was changing were the frequent fires. "Everytime I hear the fire alarm it kills me. In the past there was once in a while a fire, but now you hear it every day. In those days people used to build up their stores if there was a fire, but now they board them."

As a result of the many business closings, services people once had were lacking. "You could get everything; now all the stores are gone. You only see those restaurants which they hang around. Every store which closed and they opened they put in a restaurant." "There were six drugstores on the Avenue, now only one is left," and, according to people's evidence, even this drug-store closed at 6:00 P.M. Almost all the dentists and doctors left either because their offices were broken into or because their outside patients were afraid to come to the area. The only bank on the Avenue moved to Brookline.

The Disappearance of the Jewish Neighborhood

The main impact of the destruction of the shopping area along Blue Hill Avenue seems to be connected with the disappearance of the Jewish neighborhood. Blue Hill Avenue, according to people's recollections, was "the most beautiful Jewish shopping area you could imagine." Many typical "Jewish" stores were located along the Avenue: kosher butchers, fish stores, bakeries, delicatessens, and Jewish book stores. Most of these stores do not exist any more, and many people missed them. "You could find there all the stores you liked; Jewish food and delicatessen." "All the stores were Jewish; now it's a *churban* [devastation]." "I like Jewish fish but now there are no Jewish fish stores on the Avenue, and before *Pesach* [Passover] I couldn't get a Jewish fish. It's not important, but it annoys me that I cannot get here what I was used to." "I loved the Jewish stores, the bakery, the creamery, the fish, and the butcher. Now nothing is left here. My butcher moved to Brookline and I go to him once a month, but years ago when I suddenly wanted a piece of liver, I could get it right away." "You could buy here blinzes and white fish. What do old people who want a *chale* [white bread] do now?" It is amazing how these little things that changed matter so much to the people.

The Jewish stores did not just fulfill the daily needs of many people; they meant more than that. They were symbols of the Jewish neighborhood. Some people admitted, "There were many stores here that closed, like the butcher. We are not kosher, it's just the feeling that they were there and you could use them when you wanted."

When I did this study, three butchers were left on Blue Hill Avenue, and some people continued to shop there. "My butcher is still on the Avenue, and I drive to his store, but I'm frightened. His door is locked and he opens it only if he knows the person." Most people did not go to the butcher for that reason, and if "their" butcher was still on the Avenue, he delivered the meat to their homes.

Mattapan Square had two butchers and a bakery, but people claimed that "they are different from the small Jewish stores on Blue Hill." People complained that the butchers in the Square were expensive or did not give enough choice. The bakery also did not seem to satisfy them because "they don't bake and I don't like the bread they sell." And the delicatessen was "not like the Jewish creamery used to be." People were shopping mainly in the supermarkets, but that of course meant changing their shopping habits.

As we have seen, Blue Hill Avenue represented the Jewish neighborhood for the Mattapan people, but this was not only for the Mattapan Jews. "People would come to shop here from all over. On Thursday nights the stores were open late and it was a pleasure to go and shop. You'd meet there all kinds of people." The G&G was a kind of delicatessen plus restaurant, and very often the people interviewed mentioned it as a famous gathering place (some of them even sounded hurt when I confessed I had not heard about this place). Although there are no indications of a peer group society ever existing in Mattapan (Gans, 1962), one man mentioned "we used to meet the boys at the G&G and kibitz."

The boarded-up stores are not the only indication of the disappearance of the Jewish neighborhood. The various synagogues in the area symbolized even more strongly the Jewish identity. Although the majority of people admitted using the synagogues only on rare occasions such as the high holiday, the fact that they were there was important to them. "Jews want to be close to a *shul* [synagogue] even if they don't use it." Nothing symbolized more strongly the fact that the Jewish neighborhood had disappeared than the fact that the synagogues had closed down. "We used to go to Beith Hillel on Morton Street. When they closed two or three years ago I knew that was it. If they close

it's a sign that Jews don't live here any more." Even the few
synagogues left were not very populated. "Two years ago the
Fessenden *shul* was crowded on high holidays; last year you
could stretch on the benches." (I went to a Saturday morning
service there and counted only thirteen people.) The few people
who went to the synagogue regularly mentioned that sometimes
it is hard to find a *minyan* (the ten people needed for a service).
The safety problem also affected the synagogue: "Last holidays I
picked my mother up at the *shul* and saw a policeman in front of
the building. Who thought of this, that was the safest area!"

The fact that synagogues closed down hurt in the first place
those few people who used them regularly. "I go to the *shul* on
Woodrew Avenue. Every morning, somebody picks me up. I still
go there because I was going there all my life, and I didn't want
the *shul* ruined by them like they did with the other *shuls*. Now
they sold it. It's a beautiful *shul* but I guess that's it, you don't
have *shuls* forever."

Other Jewish institutions, although less important, are also
disappearing. "I'm a member of the Bnai-Brith chapter here. We
used to have more than 430 members, but now we have only 170.
We don't meet here any more, we meet in Hyde Park now" (a
neighborhood in Boston not far from Mattapan).

The fact that many Jews lived in the neighborhood had, of
course, a strong impact on the general character of Mattapan.
"On Friday night you knew it was Friday because everybody was
dressed up and coming home, and on a Jewish holiday the stores
were closed and you could see hundreds of people walking on the
Avenue [Blue Hill Avenue]. You knew it was a holiday; the
schools were closed here. It was beautiful." Mattapan is not a
Jewish area any more, most of the Jews and the Jewish institutions are gone, and the remaining people feel, as some expressed
it, "when I see the Avenue now it breaks my heart." Thus, the
disappearance of all these Jewish institutions symbolizes for the
Jews that Mattapan has ceased to be a Jewish neighborhood.

Changes in Mattapan Square

Mattapan Square was at the time of this study still a good shopping area. Many people, especially those who lived on the other edge of the area and did not have to pass Blue Hill Avenue on their way to the Square, admitted it. "Mattapan Square is a booming shopping area. I do all my shopping there." They claimed (and so did some of the storekeepers) that business was good and that the storekeepers were doing everything to keep it that way. The obvious change was that "you see more and more colored people in the Square," not only because blacks now lived in Mattapan, but also because "it's the only shopping center left in the whole area."

Some people, however, claimed that the Square was deteriorating. "I don't think that Mattapan Square is going to hold long. They are going out of business. I give it another year." Some claimed that "in general you see less people in the Square. Many stores are half empty." "We used to see a lot of people on the street and in the stores. From week to week you see less and less people." The Oriental Theatre, the only movie theatre in the area, closed down in 1971, and many people regarded this as another indicator that the Square was "going down." According to others, restaurants were half empty, an additional sign that the area was changing. "We went to the restaurant yesterday at 6:30. There were five people there. In the past it was so crowded that you couldn't find a place."

It is impossible to judge who was right—those who claimed the Square was "a very nice shopping area," or those who thought, "it's going down."[1] It seems that people's perception of the Square depended to some extent on where they lived in Mattapan. Those who lived north of the Square tended more frequently to believe it was deteriorating than those living south of the Square.

Whether or not the Square was still a good area, it seems

clear that the clientele had changed. On the one hand, "People from Newton used to shop at the Square but now they are afraid to come here," and on the other, "You see more and more blacks on the Square." Some claimed that "You see on the Square that the blacks are coming; there are all these funny signs on some stores which you see only in colored areas." Or that the stores were "catering toward the blacks. Once the supermarket had lots of kosher food, and now they have pork chops and things that blacks like."

The Neighborhood as a Territorial Unit

From the way people talked about the changing neighborhood, it seems clear that they used the term "neighborhood" to describe different geographical areas. As we have seen, people referred to changes on their street or in their immediate vicinity on the one hand, and to changes in the broader commercial area on the other. Both were perceived as changes in the neighborhood, although it is clear that in each case people referred to different territorial units. This brings us to the question of what constitutes "the neighborhood."

While talking about changes in their immediate vicinity, people actually referred to a very small area. The crucial thing for most people seems to be when the few houses around them changed. Although Suttles (1972) argues that this territorial unit, which he calls "face block," cannot be regarded as a "neighborhood," from the Mattapan resident's point of view the fact that blacks moved into a few houses around him is the clearest indication that "his" neighborhood changed. "My neighborhood" thus meant a few houses around one's own. "There were all Jewish families here, I mean on Messinger Street between Orlando and Favre [about five houses on each side]; I don't know who lived up the hill on the other side of the street." Those people living in the few houses around, as Suttles observed, are

seen regularly because "for any number of reasons [they] contin-
ually cross one another's pathway." (Suttles, 1972, p. 55.) People
realized that their neighborhood was changing only when the
inhabitants of the few houses around them changed. "This
neighborhood started to change about three years ago when the
first black moved onto the street. West Seldon Street [the next
street] started changing earlier, but that didn't bother us." In
many cases the changes on the next street did not even serve as a
warning. It is amazing that in spite of the fact that the area had
been changing gradually, many people indicated they did not
expect it, and, as already mentioned, were surprised that "their"
neighborhood changed. "When the first black came to Blue Hill
Avenue we didn't notice. Even when the first moved in, she lives
in the back of my house, we didn't pay attention. Only when the
family across the street sold and blacks moved in, I knew they
were here."

As we have seen, most people referred to changes in the
commercial area. These changes were important, and that was
also an indication that "the neighborhood" had changed. It is
clear, however, that although both areas were identified as "the
neighborhood," people referred to two different territorial enti-
ties. The commercial area began changing before most of the
residential area changed. Yet, in spite of the fact that people saw
blacks in the stores and at the bus stop, and knew they were
already on other streets, apparently people had to encounter
them in their daily movement, had to actually see them from
their windows, in order to perceive the change. It seems that
what is really crucial when people are talking about the changes
in "their neighborhood" are not the changes in the large area
called "neighborhood" but the changes in the immediate face
block around them.

That might be one of the reasons why The Mattapan Organization failed. When it moved into the area, trying to organize the
people in order to prevent panic selling, only 5% of the Mattapan
population was black. Although the Jews who were still there

knew that Dorchester was changing rapidly, and although many people had experienced neighborhood change before, "their" area had not started changing at that time. Most of the people interviewed had not even heard about The Mattapan Organization. It is difficult of course to judge now, but small block organizations on the changing streets might have been more effective than an overall neighborhood association.

Changes in People's Lives

The most interesting question for a study in a changing community is perhaps the extent to which these changes, as perceived and described by the people, have affected their own way of life. In other words, what is it like to live in a changing neighborhood?

Perhaps the best way to summarize the changes in people's lives is simply to say as one man did, "The main change is fear." The word "fear" was repeated again and again in the interviews: "The fear is creeping into you." "We live in fear and that's a terrible thing." "You are not safe here any more; I don't feel secure here." "You are afraid of your own shadow."

Fear, no doubt, has many impacts on people's daily lives. The major one is that people are on guard in their daily movements. They once felt free to move around, but they no longer feel that freedom. The most crucial change is that people are afraid to walk. "I don't dare to walk, not even during the day. You learn that you cannot walk here any more, I only go by car." "It's a terrible feeling that you cannot walk as much as you wish in your own country." "Whenever I go out I take a cab." Or, as a woman explained, "When I come home from work somebody has to pick me up at the MBTA station. Even when I have to walk home from the corner, I'm afraid somebody might jump on me."

Suttles' concept of the defended neighborhood might be

useful in our case. The defended neighborhood is "The residential group which seals itself off through the efforts of delinquent groups, by restrictive covenants, by sharp boundaries, or by forbidden reputation." (Suttles, 1972, p. 21.) The Mattapan Jews clearly felt that they had to defend themselves, and they limited their daily movements accordingly.

Behavioral Differences in "Good" and "Bad" Sections

Of course, not everybody stopped moving around. Some walked in spite of their fear. "I still walk to the Square, but I am scared. You cannot live in prison." No doubt in this respect there were personal differences between people. More important, however, seems to be the specific area inside Mattapan where people lived. People clearly distinguished between "good" and "bad" areas, no matter how temporary this distinction might have been. Thus, the defended neighborhood covers a different territory for various groups of people. Suttles argues that "Functionally the defended neighborhood can be conceived as the smallest spacious unit within which coresidents assume a relative degree of security on the street as compared to adjacent areas." (Suttles, 1972, p. 57.) The Mattapan Jews who lived in the "good" sections, that is, those sections which had not yet changed, felt that they could still move around freely. "This is a good street. During the day I walk. I'm not afraid to walk here."

The emphasis is on "walking during the day" because "nobody walks at night anywhere," and it does not make a difference whether one lives in Mattapan or some place else. But, "when you cannot go out of your house even during the day, it's time to move."

Several features distinguished the "good" section inside Mattapan from the "bad" one. The most obvious difference was the rate of racial change. "This street is still good; there are only a few colored here." The "bad" section was the one in which most blacks lived. There was no clear-cut physical barrier between these two sections, but people usually referred to the railroad bridge close to Mattapan Square as the dividing line. Most of those living south of the bridge felt free to walk around in the area. Yet, they knew exactly where they had to be careful. "We don't walk beyond the Square. We go to the Supreme and to the drugstore, but we won't walk on Blue Hill Avenue. When I drive up the Avenue I make sure my car is locked and my windows closed, but I don't do it in this area." Or, "This is still a good area. I don't mind walking during the day. I walk to the stores and to work. I wouldn't walk on the other side of Blue Hill Avenue." A few people who lived in the good section still walked beyond the bridge, but they tried to protect themselves. A man walking from his home in the apartment complex to the CJP (Combined Jewish Philanthropies) Center described his walk: "On Blue Hill Avenue I walk on the island in the middle of the street so that people driving by can't attack me, but I feel uncomfortable."

Since some of the Jewish people regarded the presence of blacks as one indicator of a bad neighborhood, the more blacks they saw, the more cautious they had to be. Thus, a man living in the good area described the change in his way of life. "Until a year ago I used to take a walk on the highway each night. I stopped because the area is deteriorating. Blacks started moving in here. You see them on the side streets."

There are other indicators aside from the presence of blacks which distinguish the "good" area from the "bad" one. The physical appearance of the streets is an important indicator. Piles of garbage and dirt on the streets is the most obvious sign of deterioration. The type of housing is another. Tenement housing or three-deckers which are usually in bad condition are a sign of a "bad" area. On the other hand, a clean, well-kept street with "nice" houses is in most cases considered "good." "This is a good street, it's clean and very well lit at night." And as we have already seen, the fact that Blue Hill Avenue, with its boarded-up stores, broken windows, and broken glass strewn around, looks like a "plywood city" or "ghost town," no doubt identifies it as a very "bad" area.

Crime is another important criterion which distinguishes the "good" area from the "bad" one. "This is a good street; you don't hear of crimes here. I don't know of any robberies." Connected with crime is, of course, the presence of police in the area. In the "bad" area, "You hardly see a cop," whereas in the "good" one "There is a lot of police protection; every half hour a police car is going by."

Distinguishing Safe Areas from Unsafe Areas

People developed their own private clues about where to go and where not to go. Side streets were in most cases avoided. "I used to cut to the First National Supermarket through Babson Street. Now I am walking only along Blue Hill Avenue." The "cognitive map" of safety was further broadened to elements other than territory. As we have seen, darkness was avoided in almost all cases, even if one lived in a "good" area. Although "nobody goes out at night anywhere," light still was an important criterion for safety. Dark entrances of buildings were regarded as unsafe and people tried to avoid them. (Goffman, 1971.) Some would not enter the hallway of their building at night alone. A few people even stopped using their private space after dark. "We used to have barbecues outside, now we are even afraid to sit out on the porch at night." Some people were afraid to drive alone at night, and others changed their route. "I go to town every weekend. I used to drive through Morton Street and Blue Hill Avenue. Now I come home through Hyde Park. If I had a flat tire, I'd be scared to go out of the car at 11:00 at night."

Another important criterion of safety were certain hours during the day when "dangerous" people were not around. School children, especially teenagers, were regarded as a potential source of trouble and were avoided. One Mattapan woman remarked, "I go out only in the mornings and come back before 2:30 when the kids are out of school." Yet, on the other hand, deserted streets seemed to be more dangerous than crowded ones. As another woman said, "When a lot of kids are around, like on a Sunday morning, I don't mind it so much, but when the streets are empty I am a little bit nervous." Thus, as each person had "his" defended neighborhood in which he felt safe, each developed his own private clues as to when and where it seemed less dangerous to walk.

For some people, however, Mattapan became actually not a defended but a defeated neighborhood. (Suttles, 1972.) They no longer felt safe even on their block or around their house. "I'm going to the First National, which is two minutes from here, and I'm afraid to walk. It is really ridiculous. I don't know whether to walk on the right side or on the left side of the funeral home." A few people hardly went out any more. "I'm afraid to leave the house." This was especially true for some of the old people living in the "bad" area. Some were picked up once a week by a Jewish organization, Jewish Family and Children Service (JFCS), so they could shop. Others made arrangements for deliveries. "The butcher delivers my meat; I also get my paper, my milk, and the laundry delivered. When my husband has to go to the bank in the Square, he takes a cab."

Crime and Fear

The main source of fear was, of course, the fear of crime and violence. Much of this behavior was related to bad personal experiences. As we have seen, police statistics indicated not only an increase in the overall crime rate but an increase in certain types of crime. The rate of aggravated assaults increased by 145% between 1969 and 1971 and that of robberies by 165%. The most important conclusion one can draw from these figures is that violent street crimes, that is, the more or less public types of crime, has gone up tremendously. These are the kinds of crime which are most visible and therefore noticed by the people and reported by the media. Since these are crimes which people tend to talk and hear about, from the residents' point of view the perceived increase in the crime rate might be even higher than indicated by the statistics.

Although the crime rate in Mattapan was lower than in the city of Boston in general, it was much higher than it had been. (It has been said that Police District 3 in Mattapan was the place where policemen peacefully spent their last years of service before retirement.) The nostalgic remarks of people that "years ago you could walk on Blue Hill Avenue after midnight and nothing happened to you," seem to be based on reality. It is also important to keep in mind that the rate of violent crimes was much higher in Mattapan than in places like Brookline, Newton or Milton, which were the main reference points for the Mattapan Jews. Thirty-nine of the 100 people interviewed had been victims of some crime or another in the last few years (for example, holdups, bag snatching, burglaries, and auto thefts). In some extreme cases people had been victimized more than once, as in the case of an elderly woman who told me:

> I was held up four times. The first two times they only took my money; the last two times they beat me up and threw me on the street. They cut my coat with a knife because they thought I had my money in the inside pocket. Last time I was attacked by a black at the entrance of this building. He pointed a knife at me and asked for money. He beat me. No one was around and I was scared to death. After the first two times I said to myself, "It happened twice; they only took money; it doesn't have to happen again." But now I am so scared, I'm afraid to leave the house.

Many of those who were victims of crime were old people. They are more vulnerable than younger ones. Another woman related this story:

> My husband [who was over seventy years of age] used to go to the drugstore and to other places around here. A few months ago when he came back two kids jumped on him at the

entrance of the house. They tore his trousers and took his wallet and his watch. The neighbors upstairs called the police, but what can they do? My husband doesn't walk any more; he was lucky nothing happened to him.

Some younger women also reported incidences of their bags being snatched and some were even hurt; "When you feel it on your own skin, you get scared." Bad personal experience indeed had an impact on people's behavior. "I was not afraid to walk until I was attacked. I loved to walk." Others tried to avoid the places where they had been attacked. This kind of reaction was not unique to the Mattapan Jews. A study on mugging found that "the psychological impact of having been mugged is traumatic. . . . One effect of mugging is to raise to a significant degree the victim's sense of vulnerability and mistrust." (Lejeune and Alex, 1973, p. 272.) Understandably, those people who did not seem to be frightened were those who have not been confronted with any bad experiences. "I don't feel it's dangerous as much as I hear it." Or, as somebody else concluded, "As long as nothing happens to you or to somebody you really know here, you don't get really scared."

Public Opinion and the Fear of Crime

However, bad personal experiences were not the only reason for fear and caution. Other people's experiences were also regarded as a warning signal and had an impact on behavior. "There were no crimes on this street. Now this woman has been attacked here at 7:00 in the morning when she was going to the bus stop. Since then I'm afraid to walk." Sometimes even general stories have an effect. "Until a year ago I used to walk each night to the gas station to buy a paper. I do not do it anymore. Nothing happened to me, but after all the stories you hear about this one and that one beaten up, you don't want to take any chances." The victim's need to talk about the crime and the listener's need to hear about it has been discussed elsewhere. (Lejeune and Alex, 1973.)

Rumors of crime in the area spread quickly. People heard these stories in the supermarket and in other stores, on the subway, and, of course, from neighbors. And as one woman noticed, "It goes from mouth to ear and that's bad because they get a bigger magnitude. When I came home by streetcar I used to hear, 'Did you hear of that and that?' I know people are exaggerating and I stopped paying attention to these stories." Most people, however, did pay attention to these stories.

Another source of information about crime was, of course, the media: television, radio, and especially newspapers. "You get petrified from all the stories you hear; it's on television and in the papers." Some people even complained that Mattapan gets bad publicity and that "everything that happens in Dorchester is reported as Mattapan." Exaggerated or not, the media and, above all, the printed word reinforced people's fears. One can imagine that a headline such as "Holdups turn Mattapan into a Plywood City," did not help the Jewish people of Mattapan. A few people even used to save newspaper articles on the area. The President's Commission on Law Enforcement and the Administration of Justice in its conclusion reports:

> The fear of crime may not be as strongly influenced by the actual incidence of crime as by other experience with the crime problem in general. . . . The fact is that most people experience crime vicariously through the daily press, periodicals, novels, radio and television. (1967, p. 53.)

Defending the Home

Living in fear does not mean only watching one's daily movements and limiting them to the area which one feels is more or less defended but also guarding one's home or apartment. In some cases the home itself is not regarded as a safe shelter any more. (Rainwater, 1966.)

Some of the homes in Mattapan had been broken into. "A few months ago I went to the store for twenty minutes and when I came back my house was robbed. Since then I am afraid to go out." Another woman living in a six-family apartment building in the "bad" area reported the following:

> Our apartment was robbed four times in three years. They took the television and other things. We called the owner and he put new locks on the door. The front door is locked now and nobody can come in. I got two big dogs. Nobody has robbed us since then.

In one case, a house was robbed while the woman was lying in bed. "Suddenly I saw a colored man in the house; he took my wallet with money. I screamed and he left, but I was scared to death."

The people who were robbed changed their locks, got unlisted telephone numbers, and some even installed burglar alarms. Big dogs seemed to be part of a household inventory. A fence was built around the large apartment complex and a security guard was hired after several break-ins.

The safety measures were not confined to those who had bad experiences. Others also became very cautious. "When we go out Sundays I leave the lights on because we come home late. We have double locks but we never used them until a year ago." Others would leave the radio or even the television on when they went out; a few people even claimed that that was a policeman's advice. Some people took their phones off the hook. The fear was not only of going out but also of returning home. "When I come home I stop on the stairs. I'm afraid to open the hallway door and find that somebody broke into the house." "I'm afraid to come back and to find something missing." In the past all of this was different, and some people remarked that "Years ago I used to leave everything open and go. I don't do it any more; you hear so much."

The worse fear of all seemed to be the fear of strangers. "I open the door only when I know the person. You hear on radio and TV not to open to strangers." "You can never know who is coming; you must be careful!" "You need a 'pass' to come in." The people themselves saw this as a major change in their way of life. "I used to open the door in the old days; I think it should be like that." Some old people set up a signal with those who came into their homes regularly. "The butcher and the milkman ring the doorbell three times."

The fear of strangers was so strong that sometimes the most harmless behavior was regarded as threatening and became a signal for alarm. (Goffman, 1971.) "The gas man came to read the meter. He stood there for a long time. I didn't know what he was doing there but I got scared." Some people reported getting phone calls at night without anybody speaking when they answered.

People in the "good" section of Mattapan seemed to be less on guard. They moved around more freely, opened doors more easily, and seemed to have less safety devices. Some commented that, "On this street there were no robberies, thank God!" However, even some of these people have been influenced by the stories and by the media. "I don't know why, but about a year ago somebody knocked on the door and instead of opening it, I asked through the window, 'Who is it?'"

The situation described here does not seem to be unique for Mattapan. One cannot summarize it better than the President's Commission on Law Enforcement and the Administration of Justice:

> Fear of crimes of violence is not a simple fear of injuries or death . . . but at the bottom, a fear of strangers. . . . The impact of this fear is that people stay behind locked doors of their homes rather than risk walking on the street at night. Poor people spend money on taxis because they are afraid to walk or use public transportation. Sociable people are afraid to talk to those they do not know. . . . The general level of social interaction is reduced. (1967, p. 52.)

Defending Oneself Outside the Home

A great deal of the daily activities of people were directed toward guarding their safety. It became more or less a way of life or "a state of mind," as somebody described it. Not only did people try to protect their homes, they also tried to protect themselves through various preventive "actions" which to an outsider might seem very peculiar. One of the important "rules" was not to carry money in your bag, purse, or pocketbook. "I never take a pocketbook; I take a plastic bag and just one dollar with me." "I carry the money in my pocket; I don't want to take a chance." Some people had even more "sophisticated" methods: "I don't carry a bag; I put ten dollars in my shoe." Or, "I carry the money on my body and put the charge card in my shoe. I take a bag but fill it with kleenex." The practice of carrying money in a shoe seemed to be quite widespread, and one woman even angrily told me not to mention it to anyone else when I remarked that I had heard about this "habit" from others. Some people carried "equipment" with them, such as dogs or sticks. One man said his wife and daughters used to carry tear gas in their pocketbooks.

All of these preventive measures were taken, of course, because people expected something to happen to them. The interesting point is not that they took all these precautions, but rather that they regarded them as "natural" things to do. In Mattapan any questioning of these practices (not to mention jokes) seemed out of place, and sometimes was even answered with anger. It seems that once people had gotten into the habit of playing this role, they continued to do so in an almost "natural" way. In this respect their behavior is almost like secondary deviance which "refers to a special class of socially defined responses which people make to problems created by societal reaction to their deviance." (Lemert, 1967, p. 40.) It is not clear in what way people in Mattapan learned to play this role. Some claimed nobody told them to take these measures, others admitted getting "advice" from relatives or friends, and one woman even insisted that she was told to do so by the local policeman. Wherever they learned this role, for many it became almost a way of life.

Is Crime in Mattapan Worse than Elsewhere?

There were disagreements among the Mattapan Jews as to whether crime in their area was worse than in other places. All were aware, of course, that in contrast to the good old days, crime in general was high. Many talked about the problem of law and order. "When I came to this country there was law and obedience. A policeman could arrest you if you disobeyed the law. Now the courts are liberal and the policemen are afraid to do anything." To others "the whole judicial system is bad. They protect the criminal more than the victim."

The question of whether Mattapan was worse than other places was of course relative and depended to a large extent on the people's point of reference—whether they compared their area to Dorchester or to Brookline and Newton. People had no doubts that "Dorchester and Roxbury are worse than here." Also, many people agreed that "they break into houses even in Brookline and Newton," and some even knew of people who could not get their house in Newton insured. People realized, however, that the types of crime seemed to be different. "Here there are more petty crimes, but there there are more robberies" (which, according to police records, seems to be true). Petty street crimes are more violent than crimes against property, and people are more frightened of them.

The Mattapan Jews were very sensitive to the public image of their area, and many blamed the media for this. "I think we get an unfair treatment by the media. Everything which happens here is right away reported in the papers. In Milton there are a lot of crimes but they don't release it to the papers. You don't read about it. I have a friend who lives there and they bought a burglar alarm." Some people mentioned all the "hippies around Coolidge Corner" (in Brookline) and the fact that one could not walk in Brookline either. Although most people agreed that crime was all over, and that there were robberies in other areas as well, one of their problems seemed to be that "we were never used to it here."

A minority opinion about crimes in Mattapan compared to other areas was that Mattapan had more crimes than any other place. Interestingly, the man who gave this opinion also blamed the media. "I think that the papers don't write about it any more. They try to conceal it." Most Mattapan Jews, on the other hand, did not agree with this statement.

The perception of crime depends to a large extent on people being victimized or hearing about crimes. Some claimed that crime had quieted down in the last months before the interviews, but others thought the crime rate was rising in the area. As one would imagine, those who had had recent experience of crime perceived the situation as getting worse.

Social Relations in a Changing Neighborhood

So far we have discussed the impact of the changing neighborhood on the daily life of the Mattapan Jews. Now we will deal with the effect of the changing area on their social life. There are actually two questions: social life both inside and outside Mattapan.

As we have already seen, Mattapan seemed to be a neighborhood with a loose social network. Most people were friendly with their neighbors, but, according to their recollections, they did not socialize with them in most cases. Although it might be misleading to judge social relations in the past from the present situation in Mattapan, during the four months I was interviewing daily in the area, only one woman heard about me and knew before I came to her house that I was interviewing in the area.

The fact that neighbors moved did not mean in most cases that people lost close friends. In studying the West End of Boston, Fried found that people were satisfied with their neighborhood mainly because "the residential area is the region in which a vast and interlocking set of social networks is localized."

(Fried, 1961, p. 153.) Therefore the reaction of those relocated from the area was one of grief. Mattapan, on the other hand, was an urban neighborhood with no close-knit localized social network. People had cars and it did not make much difference to them where their friends lived.

Some people reported on minor changes in their social life such as this: "We used to have a small card club, but all of the players moved out and we don't see them anymore. But most of our friends weren't in this area anyway." Those who had friends in other parts of Mattapan had to drive to see them in the past, so it actually does not make much difference for most people whether their friends are still in Mattapan or have moved out. "I still see them with the car; it's no problem."

Contact with former neighbors seemed to be quite loose. "We sometimes talk on the phone." Others saw their former neighbors in the Square occasionally. A few people even remarked that "those who left the area don't want to come back." Or that "some of your friends don't want any contact with their former friends in the neighborhood. They want to forget that they lived here. All the Jews that now live in Newton like to forget that they were once poor." But this does not seem to be a tragedy. One woman who had a few girlfriends on the street admitted that she does not see them any more. But she takes it philosophically: "They make new friends. I expect to do the same when I move."

There were, of course, some exceptions. The few people who apparently had close ties with their neighbors missed them.

> I had two good friends on the street, Stella and Ruthi. Our kids were about the same age; we played cards together in any weather, we just had to cross the street. Ruthi moved two weeks ago and Stella sold her house and will move soon. A few days ago I passed by Ruthi's house and wanted to go in. Suddenly I remembered that she left and I started crying.

The reaction of this woman was like that of the West Ender, one of grief. But she was no doubt an exception.

Fifteen people still had relatives in the area, although in most cases relatives did not live nearby and people had to drive to see them. Eight people reported that their relatives who had lived in Mattapan had left in the previous few years. Some seemed to miss these relatives very much.

The fact that in some sections only a few Jews were left did not mean in most cases that they had come closer to one another. "There are a few Jewish families on the street, but I don't socialize with them. We say hello to each other. I have a car and go everyday to the CJP Center to play cards. I don't have many friends there. The people are not my kind, but I have somebody to play with." (Only a few people interviewed visit the CJP Center regularly.) One woman, however, living on an almost completely black street, suddenly discovered a feeling of solidarity among the few Jews left: "Before, many people wouldn't talk to us. Now it's more a feeling of having something in common; they are nicer to us than in the past."

In general, what seemed to be important was not the fact that neighbors moved out and people therefore lost friends, but that they suddenly felt they "do not belong here any more." "It's not our community." What seemed to bother people was that the familiar faces disappeared and they did not know anybody anymore. "All are strangers and there is nobody to say hello to. I knew people walking on the street and recognized them, now I don't know anybody."

Changes in People's Social Life

In spite of the fact that Mattapan was not a cohesive neighborhood, social life changed for many people. In general, people went out less and therefore some met their friends less than before. A woman whose husband worked at night complained: "I'm afraid to drive to my friends at night; I go out very little now. I see my friends once a week, but not as much as I like to. You see, now that the children are grown up and I could be freer, I feel less free. All I do is watch TV and read; I put on a lot of weight and don't like it." Some who used to meet friends at the coffee shop in the Square stopped doing so because "It's almost empty; people don't like to go there." (As we have seen, the perception of the Square as a good or declining shopping area depended to a large extent on where people lived inside Matta-pan. Some who lived in the good section still met with friends at the coffee shop.)

What seemed to be the most serious problem in this respect, a problem which had a great impact on the Jews' social life, was the fact that relatives and friends were afraid to come to Matta-pan. Many people complained that their relatives and friends did not like to visit them any more. "Our relatives are afraid to visit us." I play cards, and the women are coming, but they are afraid." "My friend from Newton doesn't want to come here late because she says it's a combat area!" "We used to have a lot of parties but people are afraid to come here at night because from the outside it seems even worse than from the inside!" Suttles noticed that "the most important of these structural elements [of the defended neighborhood] is the identity of the neighborhood itself. . . . Neighborhood identity remains a stable judgmental reference against which people are assessed." (Suttles, 1972, p. 35.)

The impact of this is twofold. The most obvious is that people's social life becomes in a way limited, compared to the past. Second—and perhaps even more important—people sud-denly realize that they live in an area which is labeled as a dangerous or "combat area." They are under constant pressure from friends and relatives to move out. "All our friends and even our two daughters want us to get out." Former neighbors call and ask, "Are you still there?" All of this had a strong effect on the Mattapan people; no wonder that a woman commented, "Some-thing must be wrong with the area when you hear about all these people moving. It cannot be such a nice area if everybody is moving out."

The way outsiders reacted to the fact that people were living in Mattapan brought into focus the knowledge that it was a truly bad area, and added to their fears. People felt that "Mattapan is a dirty word." One man even admitted, "I'm ashamed to say I live in Mattapan!" Stores refuse to deliver to people in the area because "when you only say the word 'Mattapan,' people get scared. When the girl at Jordan's saw my address on the check she said 'Mattapan! You still live there?'" A woman reported that her elderly mother's doctor would not come to the house unless he called beforehand and she came down to meet him at the gate of her house. A man who owns a printing business had to deliver his goods to customers because they were afraid to pick them up. The insurance companies refused to renew policies on houses which had been broken into because they called it "a high risk area." Policemen advised people to be careful, not to carry money, and sometimes even told them not to walk on the streets. "Once we came back at night from a meeting in Hyde Park and wanted to go to the coffee shop in the Square. Two policemen saw us and said, 'What are you two doing, you should go home at this time of night.'"

One of the problems in outsiders' reactions to Mattapan seems to be connected with the fact that for them "Mattapan" is a generalized term. Yet, as Suttles noticed, "The defended neighborhood may be divided into levels or orbits which radiate from an egocentric to a sociocentric frame of reference." (1972, p. 37.) He distinguishes between the terms "my neighborhood," "our neighborhood," and "the neighborhod"—which usually possesses a name and some sort of reputation known to persons other than residents.

Outsiders ignored the fact that Mattapan was not one area, and that there were "good" and "bad" sections in this neighborhood. As one woman living in the "good" section put it, "When my girlfriends from Randolph and Brockton [a city about fourteen miles south of Boston] visit me, their husbands are worried, they think Mattapan is all one area." This is what people meant when they talked about the unfair treatment by the media.

"[Because] everything that happened near Morton Street was referred to as Mattapan."

Changes for People in Different Life Cycle Stages

As we have already seen, not all of the people had been affected to the same degree by the changing neighborhood. There were differences between people living in "good" and "bad" sections inside Mattapan. Location, however, was not the only distinguishing variable. Life cycle stage seemed to be important as well.

The Problems of the Elderly

Although sixty-six of the people interviewed were sixty years old or over and might be classified as elderly, a further distinction of age is necessary. Most people in their sixties still seemed active, many of them working. On the other hand, the people in their seventies and eighties (thirty-three of those interviewed) were confined to the neighborhood most of the time, and most of them felt the change particularly strongly (although, of course, there were individual differences).

Many changes had occurred in the lives of the old people, regardless of the changing area. Some had lost a husband or wife and were left alone. "Everything changed when my husband died a year and a half ago. Your friends leave you when you are alone." Others had gotten sick and were confined to their homes. "I do not go out much. I'm an old woman and had an operation a year ago. I'll tell you it's no pleasure to live here, it's no good any more." Or a man in his eighties explained, "I don't go out. I'm afraid I'll fall; I fell a few times on the street." Some of the elderly people lived alone, and therefore took greater safety measures. "I don't open the door. I am a woman alone and have to be careful."

Age brought about other changes in their lives. Most of the older people's friends were also old people, some of whom were sick or had died. The social network became naturally more and more limited, with people having fewer and fewer friends. "Until a few years ago people I knew from Dorchester came to play bingo. Some of them died and I got too old to set the table so I don't see the others any more." In many cases the telephone had become a substitute for face-to-face relations.

Some of the old people did not have children or had children living out of the Boston area and saw them only rarely. Although it is hard to generalize, it seems that most of those who had children in the Boston area saw them about once a week. A few claimed that their children did the weekly shopping for them. Only three of the old people interviewed had children in Mattapan.

In addition to physical handicaps and loneliness, many old people were alienated, with the feeling they no longer understand what was going on. "The whole world is changing. I don't understand it any more." They have the feeling that things are getting worse, and the phrase, "The whole world is a *churban*" (devastation) was often used by them. Changes because of age, plus the changing neighborhood, made life difficult for these old people.

Families with Children

At the time of this study, very few Jewish families with children were left in Mattapan. There were hardly any families with small children and only some with teenagers.

A common explanation of how the neighborhood began to change was "It all started with the school," referring to the Lewenberg Junior High School, which, because of open enrollment, changed its racial composition. "Lewenberg went down and families with children moved out." The quality of education was only one reason why Jewish parents refused to send their children to this school. Another reason was that parents were afraid their children might be beaten up or otherwise hurt. "The children were scared of the black kids. Parents with daughters would not let them out because the blacks would approach them."

None of the people interviewed who had teenage children (16) sent them to Lewenberg. Two families had sent their children to this school in the past, but took them out. "My daughter was beaten up by a colored girl, so I didn't send her any more to this school." The teenagers went to various schools in Boston. All parents agreed that they would not have sent their children to Lewenberg. "My older son is in the Tech. High and that's very close and convenient. If he had to go to Lewenberg, we would have left a long time ago." Those parents had the choice of sending their children to school outside the area. In one case, however, parents admitted giving a false address in order to be able to send their daughter to a school outside of Mattapan. They explained that the reason they did so was that "When they first started to bus black kids I really thought it's great that they are trying to integrate the school. They didn't integrate it; they pushed all the whites out and now it's an all-black school. I think that the school committee is much to blame."

Only a few Jewish children were elementary-school age. There seemed to be less problems with elementary schools, probably because they were more localized and one was in the "good" section. "My younger son goes here to school. It's good. There are black kids but a better element. There are enough whites to balance it." Two of the young Jewish children went to the Hebrew Day School in Milton, avoiding the neighborhood schools.

The problem of families with children was not only that of the schools. Many parents complained that their childrens' friends had moved. "All of his friends are gone." Although teenagers were not confined to the neighborhood, as were young children, their friends were reluctant to visit them in Mattapan.

In addition, there were few Jewish children in the area and

no Jewish institutions. Very frequently the parents claimed, "I'd like my daughter to have one or two Jewish friends." Or, "I'd like to have a temple and a Hebrew school so that my son can go there. He's the only Jewish child in his class." It seemed important for these parents to live in an area where their children could associate with other Jewish children. As we have already seen, one important reason that most people preferred to live in a Jewish neighborhood was because of the children. People without children would say, for instance, "Of course, it is a different story when you have children. I wouldn't live here if I had children without other Jewish kids and a Hebrew school."

It was also important for parents to raise their children in a "good" neighborhood. One woman mentioned that people do not want "to raise their children in an area of poverty," and since to her knowledge a fair number of blacks in the northern part of Mattapan were on welfare, it was a bad area to raise children.

Suttles argues that "the extent to which persons can or must concern themselves with the defended neighborhood is especially likely to vary with the life cycle stage." (1972, p. 37.) This was no doubt true in Mattapan. Old people and children and their mothers were affected more than others by the changes in the neighborhood. Thus people would comment, "I'm worried for my wife and twelve-year-old daughter who stay at home." Or a woman complained, "My husband doesn't care. He is out all day and comes home late at night." Working people, on the other hand, admitted being less affected by the circumstances. "I cannot say my life has changed much; I'm working and come home only in the evening."

Why Do They Remain in Mattapan?

In light of that stage of change in Mattapan it does not seem relevant to ask why people left the area but rather to question why they remain there. As we have seen, for many people the changes were great. For some, only their houses or apartments had not changed.

Studies of working-class neighborhoods tend to de-emphasize the importance of housing conditions. Fried and Levin claim that "most working people are not primarily concerned with the social status of their housing, and in any case their demand for housing is modest." (1968, p. 71.) The neighborhood, rather than housing conditions, is the main source of residential satisfaction. The working-class West Enders, for instance, although relocated to better apartments, were less satisfied.

In this respect the Mattapan Jews were very different from such traditional working-class people as the West Enders. In spite of their working-class jobs, they had rather middle-class values. The apartment and, more important, the house, was the major factor contributing to their remaining in the area. As some mobility studies claim, a decision to stay or leave an area seems to be influenced by the satisfaction with the dwelling unit itself. (Rossi, 1955.)

The Owners

We have already seen that most Mattapan Jews lived in good housing conditions; this was primarily true for those who owned their houses. For most home owners the house was a source of comfort and even pride. "We love our house, it's home." "We don't want to uproot and go away." "I lost a lot of money in my life, but that's not just money, that's home for me." Some simply said, "I hate to give it away." Many people invested money in their houses. "We built the basement and put in air conditioning." "I just put wall-to-wall carpets in a year ago." "We painted the house a month ago. We didn't want it to look the shabbiest on the street."

From the way people talked about their houses and "presented" one room after another, including in many cases the basement, it is clear that it was really a home to them. Unlike upper middle-class people, they intended to stay in their houses.

"We thought we'd live there for the rest of our lives." These people were aware of their good housing conditions, as well as of the advantage of owning a house and leading a more or less suburban life. "My husband likes to work in the garden." "I have a big yard and like to sit there, I like to feed the birds." People assumed that in one's own house one did not have to yield to regulations, but in an apartment, for instance, "They don't allow dogs!"

To most people moving from a house to an apartment seemed to imply "going down." "I don't want to go down and move into an apartment." "I don't like to live in an apartment after living all my life in a house." A common reason for not wanting to move to an apartment was space: "My wife has so many things. Where am I going to put them in an apartment?" "I don't want to go from six rooms to four. You have only two small closets and here I have a basement. I don't know where I'll put all my things. The furniture is dear to me and I don't want to get rid of it." Here and there people mentioned former neighbors who sold their houses and moved to an apartment and who were "sorry that they sold because they cannot get used to the place."

The problem these people faced was twofold: they did not want to "go down" in their housing condition, but they could not afford the same house in another area. "A house like ours will cost now twice as much because it's Brookline." "In a really nice neighborhood like Newton it is very expensive and we couldn't afford to buy a house there." But even in places like Randolph, houses were too expensive for many of them.

The fact that these people could not afford a house elsewhere was a sad "discovery" for some. "We were looking for another place. We didn't look seriously but asked a few real estate people. Until then we thought we are middle-class people; we have two cars, a motorcycle, a washing machine, everything. When we were looking we realized we couldn't afford a house in a nice area. Even in Milton and Randolph it's expensive. Now we can spend a dollar here or there if we want, but if we bought a house somewhere else, we couldn't do it."

Most home owners lived quite cheaply in their houses. Those who had lived there for about sixteen years would soon have finished paying their mortgage. But even those who had bought their houses more recently did not pay a very high mortgage (most around $150 a month). Even those who would have been ready to move to an apartment mentioned that a two-bedroom apartment in a better area is at least $250 a month, and they did not want only one bedroom. "Our mortgage isn't high and we live quite cheaply. We cannot afford to pay $275 a month for an apartment."

It is important to remember that these people were not young any more. Most of them were close to retirement, and therefore, as some said, "We don't want to go into great expenses in our stage of life." "We don't want to live beyond our means."

It seems that people had a choice between good housing conditions in Mattapan, or less acceptable housing conditions in a better area. For many of those owners who remained in Mattapan their houses were, at least for the time being, of greater importance.

The Renters

All of the above conditions were true for home owners. The question is why did the renters remain? Interestingly enough, renters gave some of the same reasons as owners. Many had good apartments for a relatively cheap price. For them a move would not have meant "going down" from a house but rather a less spacious apartment or paying more rent. Both possibilities did not seem very attractive. A woman in a two-family house, for instance, said, "I'll never get an apartment like this. I hate apartment buildings with many tenants where you have so little space. Here I have room closets—where will I find that anywhere else?" Or another couple confessed, "We know that for the same price we couldn't get anything like this; we'd have to take a smaller place and don't like it. So we discuss it from time to time that we want to move, but push it away." "Apartments are very expensive, around $250 per month, and we pay about half of that. I don't want to have an apartment which is less good than I have now." In addition, some of the people did not want to change their residence simply because "the idea of moving makes me sick."

There are two additional reasons why people stayed in Mattapan. First, those living in the "good" section were not under immediate pressure to move out. Those people realized that "we are still a pocket here" or that "this is the last good area in Mattapan." But at least for the moment they felt that "it's still a good area; I am not afraid to walk here." This was true for both owners and renters.

Second, a few people preferred to stay for reasons other than housing. The fact that Mattapan is in the city and has good public transportation was very important for some working people. "We have to live in the city as long as we work." "I work in Chelsea [a city on the northern edge of Boston] and don't want to live further away." "I wouldn't like to move to Randolph, it's too far for us." In an extreme case an old couple living in a very bad area had been offered an apartment in Brockton but they refused it because "we don't want to go so far." For some of these people the locational considerations were temporary, "until I retire," but at the time those were the reasons that they remained in Mattapan.

In general, however, it seems clear that good housing conditions were the main factor which kept people in Mattapan. Coleman and Neugarten in their description of lower middle-class people mention that "house and neighborhood were the cornerstones of the good life." (Coleman and Neugarten, 1971, p. 171.) Still, when people have to choose between house or neighborhood, for some it is an extremely difficult dilemma.

NOTES

1 According to the president of the Mattapan Square Merchants Association, business was good. He emphasized the fact that blacks were good customers.

CHAPTER SIX

Blacks and Jews in Mattapan

So far we have described the "dynamic" aspect of the changing neighborhood—the process of change and its impact from the point of view of the remaining Jews. The main consequence of this change is that blacks now live in the area.

In this chapter we will describe the image of the blacks held by the Mattapan Jews, the ways they distinguish between the "good" and the "bad" blacks, and the basis for this image. We will deal with the particular situation of Jews and blacks as two minority groups, and with the problems deriving from this fact. We will discuss who, from the point of view of the Mattapan Jews, is to blame for what happened in the area. We will then examine the attitude of the remaining Jews toward their black neighbors, describe the relations between these two groups, and discuss the reasons for lack of any meaningful contact between them. Finally, we will try to understand what is wrong, from the point of view of the Mattapan Jews, with the fact that blacks are living next door to them.

How Do the Jews Perceive the Blacks?

The "Good" Blacks

Most of the remaining Mattapan Jews, as we have seen, were either home owners or renters whose housing conditions were good. Very few Jews lived in the old three-deckers at the northern edge of Mattapan. The immediate contact with blacks was mainly with the home owners and to a lesser extent with the tenants in the new apartment buildings. In other words, the black neighbors were in most cases the "good" blacks.

This fact seems to be important. The Jews did not regard all blacks as one unified category and made a clear distinction between owners (plus renters in the expensive apartments) and renters. Lacking in most cases any other criteria to judge the blacks in the area, the type of housing became the major reference point for evaluation. As other studies have indicated (Warner, 1949; Coleman and Neugarten, 1971), housing is a very important component of status.

The Mattapan Jews assumed that "Those who can afford such a house must be of the better class; the homes here are $30,000." "They are home owners, people who worked for their house all their life. Both husband and wife are working. If they could buy a house, they must be respectable." Thus, from the fact that blacks own a house one can learn many other things about them. "They must have some kind of job if they can afford such a house. They aren't on welfare. They are educated. Even if they are workers, they must have a better standing; they have a steady job. They don't have nine children."

Some people knew what their black neighbors did for a living. A few even mentioned that the blacks were professionals. "They are of higher class. One is an accountant. A woman who lives here is a chemist at Polaroid Company." That is, however, not the crucial point. What was important was that the blacks were not on welfare, had a steady job, and were therefore "respectable." "I'm sure RCA wouldn't employ him if he were a bum."

Most Mattapan Jews had only a vague idea of what their black neighbors did, but that did not bother them. The type of house and the neighborhood was in itself an indicator of their social standing. "If they were real professionals they would have lived in Newton or a place like that. But the people here are not on welfare, otherwise they couldn't afford to buy these houses." The fact that blacks owned houses was an indication of their social and even moral characteristics. "I don't say that rich people are always good, but they must work and that means that they have a job. Nobody is going to hire them if they were nobodies."

One point must be added here. Most people, especially home owners, had at least some idea about FHA mortgages the blacks received in order to buy homes. They knew that only a few hundred dollars was needed for a down payment. So, the criterion for "respectability" is not only the fact that blacks can afford to buy a house but also the way they keep it. Thus, the way people keep their property and not only the fact that they own it becomes an important clue for evaluating them. "They are very nice and you should see how they take care of their property." "Some of them are very nice, like those who live on my street. They are clean, they keep their property very well." "They are not the bums, they keep their property very well, they are fussy about their home."

A house for the black home owner, as for the Mattapan Jews, was a source of pride, and the Jewish people paid attention to this fact. "They take pride in their houses, you can see it." "You can tell it's the first time they've owned a house the way they cut the lawn." Some even admitted that "they keep their homes beautifully, I'll tell you better than the Jews who lived there before."

The implications were even greater than this. The way blacks kept their houses was not only an indication of their values but also of their economic position. "O.K., the government helped them to buy the house, but they need money to keep it as they do. So they aren't the cheaper ones, not the *raffniks* who live in Dorchester." People attributed many other characteristics to the home owners who kept their property well. In addition to being "nice" people, they were regarded as clean, quiet, and hardworking. They "want to better themselves," and what seems to be most important in the eyes of the Jews was that "they want to give their children a better education and give them a chance in a better place." Some, especially the few Jews who had children, noticed that "the children are well behaved, they teach them not to get in trouble."

There were some exceptions. A few people noticed bitterly that "even welfare cases could come and buy here." The two people who said that also thought that the blacks did not take care of their property. "My neighbor doesn't take care of his property; he got it for nothing. A door was broken a few.months ago and he hasn't fixed it yet. That's enough for me to know what kind of person he is." Thus, the way people keep property can also indicate their "bad" characteristics.

That was a minority opinion, however; the general agreement was, as one man summarized it, "In general, you can say that those who own their houses are a different kind of people; they keep up their property; they worked hard for it and value it. They have respect." The same reasoning, that is, that money is a sign of respectability, also applied to the renters in the new, fairly expensive apartment buildings. "If they can afford to pay such a rent, they must be nice."

The "Bad" Blacks

Most Mattapan Jews agreed that "the trouble is with those who live in the three-deckers," referring to the renters who occupied the old apartment buildings in Dorchester and the northern part of Mattapan. They were regarded as aggressive, rough, lazy, dirty, arrogant, and even immoral. To illustrate this point the following are some of the characteristics the Mattapan Jews attributed to the "bad" blacks, or, in other words, "the trash." "They are fresh and want money in the easy way, instead of working they rob and hold people up." "The bad ones steal and rob and knock down old people. They drink, they don't work, and don't have family life. You can see a lot of women with children." "Wherever they come it's so dirty." "They smell and drink." "They have this habit of eating on the street and throwing out the garbage." "They make a lot of noise." "They are arrogant and ignorant and ruin everything." "They are arrogant. You can see it in the way they drive, they don't give you the courtesy of the road. You can see it on their faces, as if everything is coming to them." "They are pushy and want everything first, when they drive they always have to be before you." Some of the Jewish adjectives used to describe the "trash" are *mamserim* (bastards), *wilde chayes* (wild animals), and *schmutz* (dirt). In sum: "They are trouble."

The "bad" blacks were those "coming recently from the South because of the welfare." One lady saw the situation this way: "They get off the bus and get the welfare payment, so why should they work? They get money for each child and make eight or nine children." In contrast to those coming from the South, there were the Bostonian blacks, regarded in most cases as the "good" ones. "When I grew up in Roxbury there were a lot of colored people there but they were different." "There was no trouble. That was before the civil rights period."

Another distinction made between "good" and "bad" blacks was that of age. "The old generation blacks are O.K., but the younger ones are fresh." A middle-aged man working in a machine shop where 60% of the workers were blacks observed, "An old black will step aside when I pass; a young one will wait till I step aside."

The image of the "bad" blacks as being troublesome was

reinforced by the attitude of the "good" blacks toward them. At least that is the way the Mattapan Jews saw it. "They are running away from their own people." Some noticed that their black neighbors sent their children to private schools because they did not want them to go to school with the "trash." One woman recalled a conversation between her two black neighbors, and claimed that one said to the other, "It's time to move, the Niggers are coming!"

It is impossible from our data to judge whether the Jews' impressions of their black neighbors are true or false. Yet, some of the activities of various black neighborhood groups, directed to preserve the area as a good community, could also be interpreted by the Jews as an effort to keep lower-class people out of the area. For instance, some neighborhood groups organized black residents to patrol their streets. Also, these groups opposed additional liquor stores in the area.

The main complaint Jews had against blacks was that they were violent and aggressive. Many Jews no doubt think what one expressed: "I'd say most of them are riff-raff." A sixteen-year-old boy described the blacks in his high school class this way: "There are some colored boys from Roxbury, they are very aggressive. I think it's because they do not have a good family life. They are rough. If you meet five kids, you don't know what they will do to you." Some believed that the reason blacks were aggressive is that "they were oppressed so long and got loose all of a sudden."

One of the popular themes people discussed in the interviews was whether blacks commit more crimes than whites. The Mattapan Jews differed in their opinions. Some thought blacks always committed more crimes than whites. "There are more colored than whites who do all these things." "Seventy-five percent of the crimes are done by blacks, mainly from Dorchester and Roxbury." "They hold up and rob more, although whites are learning from them." On the other hand, other people claimed that "blacks and whites commit crimes, it is in this area it happens to be more blacks because they live here." "Whites also commit crimes, only in this area I think most crimes are committed by black kids."

The Basis of This Image of Blacks

Why do the Jews have such an image of blacks? How do they know that blacks are aggressive? The fact is that most of the Mattapan Jews did not really know any black people. They judged blacks from what they heard and saw. The clearest indication for the Jews that blacks are violent is that blacks themselves say so. "They even say it on television that they'll kill the whites." "They hate the white man, they want to kill him, they say it on television. Their organizations preach hate." "They are brought up to hate and that's what they are taught. If one of them does something wrong, they won't punish him. They stand for each other. They call him brother."

Thus, the ideology of the more militant groups among blacks is perceived by many Jews as the common ideology of most black people. In a survey in New York City, Harris found that 45% of the Jews interviewed believed that the blacks "want to tear down white society," compared to only 20% of the blacks themselves. Harris concludes that "The Jewish group in N.Y.C. has developed some serious misapprehensions about the notions and intentions of the black community." (Harris and Swanson, 1969.) As we will see later, not all Mattapan Jews share this belief.

Another alleged proof that blacks are violent, aggressive, and hateful is "the way they behave and the way they look at you." "I don't want to get near them the way they look at you. They are taught hate; their organizations teach them hate." "They look at your face as if you owe them something; better housing, education, everything." "They are not refined people. You can see it in the way they look at you. They push everybody aside." A lonely woman who used to walk on the street and just smile at people described it this way: "You walk along Almont Street and see all the colored faces on the porches. It's the way they look at you. They don't say it, but you know they think, 'Don't smile at me white man, we know what *you* feel, you are not as good as us.' It's like a vibration in the air, you feel it on your skin."

Many Jews claimed it was not just "the way they look at you," but also the way blacks talked. Jews having occasional contact with blacks in stores very often complained that they were not polite. "I went to the laundry the other day and it was full of colored people. The way they look at you with such hate, it's frightening. I asked one of them if I could put my things in the washing machine and she answered in a rude way, 'Wait until I finish.'" Some people commented that the blacks walk around "as if they have a chip on their shoulder."

To the Mattapan Jews, perhaps the strongest indication that blacks were violent and ruined everything was "What they did to Blue Hill Avenue." We have already discussed the changes on Blue Hill Avenue. The Jews blamed the blacks for the fact that "Blue Hill Avenue looks like a *churban* [devastation]." "Look what they did to the stores on Blue Hill Avenue. They ruined everything; they burned down the stores; they ruined the apartments. They think that because they were enslaved they must pay back, but this doesn't make sense." "The blacks took over all the stores. People have to leave. They threatened them that they'll burn them." "The owner of the bookstore didn't want to give them the money for protection, so they shot him. He's lucky he's alive. . . ."

The final proof that blacks took over the stores only to force people out and to ruin everything is the fact that, as people put it, "They cannot run a business." "The colored took all the stores, but what did they do with them? The TV repair is gone and also other stores. I'm asking you, why can't they handle a store?" Or another example: "A few months after they took over the G&G, they ran out of business. They got the Ford agency and after a month one hundred cars were stolen." The conclusion people drew from this was that the blacks' only purpose was to force the storekeepers to leave so that they could "take over" the place.

The Fear of the Blacks

This image of "bad" blacks led to one result, that of fear. It is quite obvious that a large number of the Mattapan Jews were afraid of blacks. "Whites are afraid of *schwarze*, but *schwarze* are not afraid of whites." Many shared the belief that "the colored are more dangerous than whites." A woman tried to explain her attitude toward blacks by saying, "I'm not prejudiced, I'm just scared."

Black teenagers were regarded as particularly dangerous. "When I see a gang of colored kids, I'm petrified. I don't know what they are up to." "I see the riff-raff around and that's scary." Some tried to protect themselves: "When I see a group of colored teenagers, I go to the other side."

Are black teenagers more dangerous than white ones? Many Jews in Mattapan said that this was the case and that they would pay no attention to a group of white youngsters. A few people explained that they were not used to colored people. "I did not see a colored till I came to this country." Some, on the other hand, put it in a different light. "I get scared only if I see a group of colored kids and they look at you as if they are up to something. I don't see here groups of white kids; if I'd see them, I'd probably be scared too."

The fact that most bag snatchings and other petty crimes in the area were committed by blacks reinforced the fear of blacks in general. As one woman explained it, "If something happens to you once, you generalize. Each black I see I think he is up to something." One of the reasons people generalized about blacks is, as some said, "to me all look alike. I cannot tell one from another." In other words, it is difficult to distinguish between the "good" and the "bad." As we have seen, the major distinction was between home owners and renters. Nevertheless, this is not enough when one has to distinguish between those two groups on the street. People need further clues in order to know with whom they are dealing. Opinions in Mattapan were divided about whether it is possible to distinguish between the "respectable" blacks and the "trash." Those who claimed one can distinguish between the two groups said that "you can see it in the way they talk and behave." Dress also seems to be another indicator. (Suttles, 1968.) "You can see it in the way they behave and dress and even look. Look how they walk and dress."

On the other hand, there were others, and they seemed to be the majority, who thought that "you cannot tell who is nice and who is not; you don't even know who are those who will do something to you and who are the nice ones." Therefore, "You better not take chances." The trouble is, of course, that when people think they cannot distinguish between the "good" and the "bad" blacks, they are suspicious of every black they meet. One woman described an incident which explains this point:

> Two sisters were walking in front of the CJP Center. Suddenly they saw two colored fellows and one said to the other, "Be careful." But she answered, "They are dressed nicely, nothing can happen." And they beat her up! Her sister had to take her to the hospital. Even those who are nicely dressed are doing these things!

Victims of mugging elsewhere also reported that appearances were deceiving. (Lejeune and Alex, 1973.)

We have described at length the image the Jews have of the "bad" blacks. It seems important to emphasize again that the Jewish people in Mattapan did not consider all blacks as aggressive, violent, and hateful. They made a clear distinction between the "good" blacks, that is, the respectable home owners who lived in their neighborhood, and the "bad" blacks, the renters in the old three-deckers. Several times people repeated, "It's only the bad element which come here and cause trouble which bother me."

The remaining question in this context is whether the "good" blacks were regarded as an exception or minority or vice versa.

Again, opinions were divided. Many of the Mattapan Jews thought that their nice black neighbors were a minority. "There are good and bad ones, but those who have anything to do with them, think that many are bad." "There are also bad whites, but the majority of *schwarze* are bad." "Not all blacks are bad. I have some colored friends from the Handel and Hayden Society. I invite them to parties, but I think they are an exception." "There are some good blacks but most of them are not educated."

Others said that "you have bad whites too and not only bad blacks; you have even bad Jewish people." "There are good and bad blacks, but that's also true among the whites." "I don't say all blacks are bad, but a handful of them spoil it for all of them. Senator Brooks is a good man; Elma Lewis [a black leader] is good; but some of them are bad." This view was best summarized by a woman who said, "For five bad blacks there are probably a hundred good ones, but the image of the blacks is that of the slum people." And, therefore, as somebody else suggested, "You cannot blame all blacks for what a handful are doing."

Blacks and Jews as Two Minorities

The fact that Jews are also a minority group explains the ambivalent attitude many of the Mattapan Jews share toward the blacks. On the one hand, the Jewish people resent the fact that the blacks are given benefits they had to work hard for; on the other hand, they sympathize with them.

Blacks, Jews, and the Welfare System

The Mattapan Jews inevitably compared themselves with the blacks. "Blacks get everything they want. Jews came here with nothing, but they were ambitious and worked themselves up." "Today they get everything because they are colored. They demand things we didn't dare to ask for and if they don't get it, they say discrimination." Some expressed a bitter memory of the past: "Years ago only those who worked got money. During the Depression there was no welfare. Jews had charity but no welfare. Now the more they demand, the more they get. Everything has changed."

The strong resentment of the Mattapan Jews toward welfare is understandable in view of their "Protestant-Jewish" work ethic. These people worked hard all their lives and believe that those who work are rewarded. They discussed this subject again and again during the interview.

> Today everybody talks about the underprivileged, but it has no meaning. The fact that you are poor doesn't mean that you cannot be decent. Jews were also poor and they are still, but they worked hard for all that they got. Today those who are on welfare demand everything and get it, and I think that's not right.

Or, somebody else commented, "Half of the state's budget goes to welfare and that's ridiculous. Who helped the Jews? They helped themselves! Why don't they do the same? Jews were too proud to ask for anything." The solution in the eyes of some Jewish people was expressed this way:

> They shouldn't get welfare and go to work. My father worked very hard when he arrived. They get everything and don't want to work. When you see them in the supermarket they buy the most expensive things. They don't even look at the prices. They spend fifty or sixty dollars like nothing because they get it so easy. They drive the most expensive cars.

Jews were not only poor and worked themselves up, but, according to the Mattapan people, also were—and to some extent still are—discriminated against. "Jews were also discriminated against but they didn't cause trouble." (In the Harris survey, 45% of the Jews in New York City felt that Jews are discriminated against. The lower the socioeconomic status, the greater the feeling of discrimination.) A few even felt that they were discriminated against compared to the blacks. As one man saw it, "They say they have been discriminated against but that's not true. I went with some of them to school. They are doctors and lawyers and I am a cab driver."

Many of the Jews living in the non-Jewish section of Mattapan sometimes described the hostile reaction of their gentile neighbors when they first moved into the area. "It took a long time until the Jew proved himself, until he made it, until the *goyim* [gentiles] learned that the Jew isn't dirty. But they [the blacks] want to get everything at once." Or, "The Jews were also not wanted but they behaved well. My neighbors realized that not all Jews are loud and dirty." Many recalled the fact that until recently Jews could not buy a house in Milton because in "Yankee City" they did not want Jews.

A few people felt the help blacks got in housing was unfair. Comparing himself to the blacks, one man remarked, "I worked twenty-three years for my house and they got it for nothing." One woman even concluded, "The blacks who get the houses don't earn it. Jews were also a minority and even today there is discrimination, but did they ask for anything? If they cannot afford a house, they shouldn't buy it. Everybody should have what he can afford. If they can afford to rent only a one-room apartment, they should do so."

In a way it is understandable that the Mattapan Jews resented the welfare and the help blacks got in housing. These working-class and lower middle-class Jews felt they worked hard and just made it. The realization that others got the same things they worked so hard for "for nothing" almost shattered their value system. The welfare system plus the problems of law and order led some people to believe that "everything is bad now."

Nevertheless, the fact that the Mattapan Jews resented the welfare and the way blacks were treated does not mean that they were not sympathetic to them. Even most of those who complained about the welfare system realized that blacks have been oppressed and discriminated against. Only a small minority, such as the cab driver quoted above, felt there was no discrimination. People would make remarks such as "I can understand them in a way. They were oppressed so long. But the way they behave is horrible." Most Mattapan Jews were clearly ambivalent in their attitude toward blacks. "I feel really bad about it; I'm really not bigoted. I wouldn't want to know that my grandmother was a slave; but why do they have to ruin things?" Some emphasized the fact that because Jews are a minority, they can understand the blacks better. "I know they have been discriminated against, and as a Jew who suffered I know what it means." "Black people have the right to have a house, I know what it means when you cannot find a decent home."

Are the Blacks Anti-Semitic?

How did the Mattapan Jews perceive the blacks' attitude toward them? In other words, do blacks hate Jews more than other whites? The Mattapan Jews had some opinions on this subject. Most people interviewed claimed, "They hate whites, period. But they hate more those whom they are in contact with." Blacks are close to Jews, and, therefore, Jews "suffer" more because of blacks than other whites do. This fact was repeated by many of the Mattapan Jews. "They hate those which are closest to them. They live in Jewish areas. I would think that two minorities would get along together, but that isn't so. They are anti-Semitic. They don't do it to the *goyim* [gentiles]."

Some Jews claimed that they had to "pay" for being liberal. "Of course they are anti-Semitic, the only contact they have is with Jews. Jews were more liberal than other groups. The Jewish landlords let them into their houses, the storekeepers were the last ones who remained in the ghetto." "I really don't understand why the colored people pick on the Jews; Jews helped them so much—they are also a minority and suffered. They pick only Jewish areas." One woman even commented, "It's like you spoil a child and he gives you back." A few even had the feeling that Jews were scapegoats. "They hate whites in general, but they have more contact with Jews so they blame them for everything. They ruined the Jewish neighborhoods all over the country." "It was like a *Shtetl* [a small town in Eastern Europe where Jews used to live] and they destroyed it." The burning of the synagogues was also regarded as proof of black anti-Semitism.

The Mattapan Jews shared the widespread belief that "blacks follow Jews." Most of them lived in Boston for the greater part of their lives and were aware that "you won't find a black in South Boston or in the North End, they'll kill them." As most of these people previously lived in Roxbury and Dorchester, they were able to speak from personal experience. "I was born in Roxbury and lived more or less all my life in the same area. Wherever I moved always blacks followed us." Some explained that blacks move into Jewish areas because they know that "Jews will leave. They won't fight back and run away." It is interesting that one of the explanations of why gentiles sometimes are hostile to Jews entering their neighborhood is that "They know when Jews come, blacks will come after them."

Very few of the Jewish people regarded black anti-Semitism as related to religious factors. "They hate Jews for two reasons. One, they are not gentiles, and all *goyim* always hate Jews; and, two, they are white." Although, as we have seen, many Jews believed that Jews were (and even to some extent still are) discriminated against—"*Goyim* don't hate Jews?!"—many thought that black anti-Semitism is worse than white anti-Semitism. The reason was, as Jews see it, that blacks were more violent and aggressive than gentiles. "*Goyim* will hate you, but won't kill you."

From studies dealing with blacks' attitudes towards Jews, the Mattapan Jews' perception of black anti-Semitism seems to some extent exaggerated. Marx found that blacks did not hate Jews more than they hated other whites. "Jews are by and large not singled out as being worse than other whites, nor are they seen as generally better than other whites." (Marx, 1969, p. 138.) Harris in his New York City survey found that "Jews tend to believe that black anti-Semitism is worse than in reality." (Harris and Swanson, 1969, p. 117.) Marx also compared his findings to others and concluded that "Negroes do not appear to be higher in anti-Semitism than other whites." (1969, p. 147.)

Not all Mattapan Jews thought that blacks were anti-Semitic. Some simply said they "don't have any reason to." Others provided alternative explanations for blacks' attitudes towards Jews, such as, "I don't think they hate Jews more than other whites; there is a similarity between them; both are minorities, but I think they are jealous of them." A few admitted that Jews might have exploited the blacks, but they added that it was not only the Jews who exploited blacks. The ambivalence of the Jews' attitudes regarding this point can be learned from the following quote. "Some of them might hate Jews, and they say they have reasons for it. Jews hired blacks and gave them very low salaries. On the other hand, nobody but the Jews would hire a black."

Who Is to Blame for What Happened?

The Mattapan Jews, as we have seen, believed that "blacks follow the Jews" and only the Jews. As proof of this they often mentioned that their neighborhoods changed while others did not. People often asked themselves how all this happened and, why had their area changed? In other words, they often wondered whose fault it is that their neighborhood, which used to be "the most beautiful Jewish community you can think of," is "not our community any more."

The Jewish Organizations

The Mattapan Jews were aware of the fact that they did not belong to the Jewish upper middle-class mainstream, at least as it is represented by the Jewish establishment. Their resentment toward the Jewish organizations and their liberal attitude toward blacks seems understandable. Some put it this way, "I think that those who try to help them [the blacks] and are very liberal don't have much contact with them." They feel that "Jews are catering to the blacks," and instead of helping poor Jewish people are helping the blacks. "I think the Jewish organizations made a big mistake by supporting the black organizations. Why do Jews have to take care of the whole world? Don't they have enough problems of their own? There are enough Jewish poor to spend the money on."

Some people were very angry with the Jewish organizations in Boston because they sold a deserted synagogue in Dorchester for $1 to a black organization represented by Elma Lewis. They felt that "They shouldn't have given Elma Lewis the Mishkan Tefila *shul* for one dollar. I think she doesn't appreciate it. I saw her on television." Continuing this subject, somebody else added, "What did they do with the Mishkan Tefila? They ruined it. All the windows are broken."

The resentment toward the liberal attitude of the Jewish establishment was sometimes not limited to the local organizations but was seen in a wider context. "I was very angry when the rabbis marched to Mississippi. They should have done it in their name, not in mine. I don't want to be part of it. I think the Jews did too much for blacks and too little for their Jewish brothers."

The role that the Jewish organizations played in the process of the change in Mattapan, according to the Jews there, is not clear. Some claimed that the Jewish institutions could not do anything "because you cannot convince people not to panic when they saw what happened on Blue Hill Avenue. When people are panicky, nothing will stop them." A few thought that the organizations were afraid to intervene because "If they had said anything, it would be as if they were anti-black, and they didn't want others to think that they were anti-black."

Other people, on the other hand, claimed that "the Jewish organizations could have done something, but they didn't. If they would have explained to people that everyone who moves away makes it worse for those who stay, that might have helped." (As already mentioned, the Mattapan Organization was active in the area in 1968–69. Most people interviewed, however, did not know of this organization.) Some blamed the local leadership, for example, the rabbi "who left to go to the rich Jews in Newton." A few observed that "When we went on the last high holidays to the *shul*, the rabbi said we shouldn't leave, but he was already leaving. How could he be such a hypocrite?"

A few even accused the Jewish organizations of not caring about the Mattapan Jews. "They wrote Mattapan off because it was an aging community and money didn't come from here. They invested in other places like Newton and Randolph where younger people live." Another comment was, "I think that the Jewish organizations instead of demonstrating for Soviet Jewry, should have demonstrated against this."

Whether the Jewish organizations could have done anything or not, the fact remains that they had very little contact with blacks. At least that is the way the Mattapan Jews saw it. "The people of the CJP live in Newton where there are no blacks." Therefore, some people questioned their moral right to interfere in this situation. "I'd like the Jewish Philanthropies instead of talking that they [the blacks] are nice people and there is nothing wrong to live with them, to come and live here. But instead they are going far away to Newton and Framingham [a city about 17 miles south of Boston]."

The Jews Who Left Mattapan

Nevertheless, the Jewish organizations are not solely to blame for what happened in Mattapan. The remaining Jews realized that if the others had not sold, the area would not have changed. Some recalled that long before the blacks moved into the area, the younger people moved to the suburbs with the help of GI loans and other mortgages because Mattapan "wasn't good enough for them any more." According to this view, Jews always wanted to "better themselves" and "they always have to move to newer areas. Newton is a Jewish ghetto. The first thing Jews ask you is 'Where do you live?' and they judge you by the neighborhood which you are in." Others, being more charitable, admitted that when young Jewish people reached the stage of buying a house, they preferred the suburbs for many good reasons. In any case, Jews are not only more liberal than gentiles, according to the Mattapan Jews, but also more mobile. The result was that those who were left behind in the area were to a large extent the elderly.

The realization that "blacks follow the Jews" and that blacks move primarily into Jewish neighborhoods leads many people to believe that Jews sell their property and run away more easily than gentiles. "Jews get panicky and run away, they don't fight back." Some people were, nevertheless, sympathetic to those who sold. "I don't blame the people who sold, they were all elderly who were scared by crime and by the real estate people." "They were terrorized by the blacks." Interestingly, only a few people mentioned that those who left did so because they were bigoted.

Others were not so sympathetic, blaming the Jews who sold for what happened:

> It's all the fault of the Jews, they are greedy, they want to make money. For a few dollars they sold their houses. Of course they made money. My landlady bought the house for $10,000 and sold it for $25,000! Now they cry that they have been pushed out of here. They brought it on themselves. They said, "I saw the writing on the wall," but I tell you our Jewish people, God bless them, want to make money!

Not surprisingly, this view was expressed by renters rather than owners. People tried to find explanations of why Jews sell more easily than gentiles. Some were unable to explain it. "To tell the truth, I don't understand why they run away. Let's say you have twenty-five houses on the street and two are black ones, what can they do to you? They are still a minority."

Some Jews observed that gentiles are less mobile than Jews. Sometimes they live in the same house for over a generation. People gave various reasons for the residential stability of their gentile neighbors. They want to live near the church; their leadership is stronger than that of the Jews; or education is not quite so important to them and, anyway, they send their children to parochial schools. (Some of these reasons were mentioned also by the Catholic priest.) Jews, on the other hand, "were all their life wandering, they didn't stay in one place."

Housing conditions themselves are regarded as another reason for residential stability. Gentiles live in older houses than Jews and will not lose as much money. "Jews have better houses. They bought them ten or twenty years ago and paid about $20,000. The *goyim* have older houses which cost at the time only about $7,000. Naturally, they have less to lose than the Jews." According to this view the difference is mainly an economic matter.

According to the Mattapan Jews, the belief that Jews panic and run away was shared by their non-Jewish neighbors. "My Italian neighbor is selling now. He said he'd never go to a Jewish area because Jews are spoiling the area for him." People claimed that they heard remarks such as "My friend told me not to buy in a Jewish area because they are the first to sell to blacks." The impression that Jews sell more easily raises some doubts among the Jewish people themselves about whether it is desirable to live in a Jewish area. "I thought it's good to live in a Jewish area because you are used to living among your own kind. Now I don't know. I see all the Jews selling but gentiles in this area don't sell."

Not all the Mattapan Jews shared the opinion that Jews were running away and gentiles were staying. According to this view it was a matter of time. Gentiles lived mainly in the southern part of Mattapan, which began changing only recently. "Now also the *goyim* are selling. The Portuguese woman across the street is moving out and is renting to *schwarze*." (According to FHA records, many sales in 1972 were in the non-Jewish section of Mattapan.)

The Establishment

The Jews themselves were only partly responsible for what happened in Mattapan. The major blame, according to the Mattapan Jews, lies with "them." "They" are, beside the Jewish organizations, mainly the banks, the FHA, the real estate people, the city, and the politicians—in other words, the establishment. The stories in the Boston papers were well known to the Mattapan Jews, and they interpreted them in their own way. (The *Boston Globe* published a series of articles about Mattapan.)

> Twenty-one bankers got together, eighteen of them Irish, and decided to give blacks mortgages in this area. They could get it for nothing, just a few hundred dollars! Even welfare cases could buy here. The brokers heard about it and started to scare the people that their property values is going to drop. We also got a letter!

Many referred to the real estate people and the block busting. "They did a lot of harm." Some even mentioned that the word "Mattapan" had become a synonym for block busting.

People's main complaint was that Mattapan had been the only area chosen for the blacks. "I blame the FHA and the banks for the 'red line.' They shouldn't have zoned this area." To most people it seemed a deliberate act and, in a few cases, even a "plot" of the policy makers. "The banks got together and decided to ruin the neighborhood. I think they did it to prevent riots, but Boston didn't have much riots." "I think the whole thing was done deliberately. Of course the colored people should have a place to live, but why put them all here? Why didn't the politicians put them on Beacon Hill?" "They need a place to live, I know that. They tore down all the old houses in Roxbury and didn't build new ones. But they shouldn't have made this the only area for them. There should be blacks everywhere, but not the whole area as it is now."

Another question the Mattapan Jews raised is why the FHA mortgages were only available to blacks. "I think that the banks did a very bad thing in giving the three percent mortgages only to blacks and in certain areas. They should have given the mortgages to everyone and everywhere." The reason blacks got the FHA mortgages is, in the view of some Jews, because "The politicians want their vote and they cater to them. You know how we call Mayor White, 'Mayor Black!'" Some mentioned the fact that the local politicians do everything for the blacks. "When our kids were small there was nothing on the playground. Now you must see the new lights they put on the Almont and Norfolk playgrounds! They do it only for them."

> They ruined our neighborhood, the city, the FHA. Why did they do it to us? Why did they choose this area? O.K., they want to give them mortgages, but they should have told them they can buy where they want. We have representatives; why didn't they fight for us? Mrs. Sargent, I'll tell you, she's a lot to blame. But she doesn't live here and White doesn't live here either.

In short, the fault of what happened lies, in the eyes of the Mattapan Jews, in "the system." People's reaction, as demonstrated by the quotes, was a mixture of anger, pain, and helplessness. The way they saw it, only the working and lower middle-class Mattapan Jews suffered because "the rich Jews who sold first didn't lose money. They had connections with the real estate people and with the city. The rich people knew what was going on!"

The Mattapan Jews, very much like the "Middle Americans" (Coles, 1970), found themselves caught in the middle; between the blacks, and especially the "trash" threatening to invade their neighborhood, and "the system," which is to blame for what has happened.

Contact with Blacks

Until now we have dealt with the image of the blacks and with the Mattapan Jews' attitude toward blacks rather than with the actual relations between those two groups. Yet, most Mattapan Jews had black neighbors and the contact with them seemed to be a very real issue. In the northern part of Mattapan, where only a few Jews live, they are a visible minority among their black neighbors. On those streets, which are in the process of change,

Jews and blacks lived side by side. Only a few Jews lived on streets that blacks have not yet moved onto, and thus they did not have black neighbors.

What are the relations between Jewish and black neighbors in Mattapan, and what is the impact of residential contact on the attitude of the Jews toward blacks? We have already seen that most Jews regarded their black neighbors as "nice" and "respectable." "Not like the trash living in Roxbury and Dorchester." Although most Jews had only a vague idea of the blacks' exact professions, many Jews were impressed by the socioeconomic status of their neighbors and emphasized the fact that they probably had steady jobs and good salaries. One woman described her black neighbors: "I'm sure they are making a few hundred dollars a week; he works for the state and she is a nurse." Although all my information about the Mattapan blacks derives from the Jews, and it is hard to know how accurate it is, it seems that the socioeconomic status of the blacks is at least as high as that of the Jews. (According to the 1970 census, the median income of the Mattapan blacks was $8,779 compared to $9,552 for the white— Jewish and non-Jewish—population.)

At least in this respect Jews and blacks fulfilled one of the four characteristics which are essential for successful interracial contact, that is, equal status. (Allport, 1958.) This point is important. The Social Science Panel of the Advisory Committee to HUD in its report emphasizes that

> At present the desirability of intentions to foster socio-economic mixing in residential areas is uncertain. In question are not only the possible benefits, but untested assumptions concerning the amount and kind of present interaction across socio-economic lines. (1971, p. 54.)

Despite the almost general agreement among Jews that their black neighbors were of "the better class," relations with black neighbors were another matter. For most people, contact with black neighbors was limited. "I have two black neighbors on the floor. We say 'hi' and that's it." Or, "We don't bother them and they don't bother us." Some people reported talking with their black neighbors on the street or beyond the yard. In some rare instances a few people reported that "yesterday my neighbor came in and I showed him the house." Or a Jewish tenant whose black landlord lives downstairs remarked, "On Christmas I went down for a drink."

The most common type of relation was almost no relation at all. There was, of course, a visual contact between the two groups since there was no territorial segregation between Jews and blacks. This lack of relations has also been found in a study of 200 integrated neighborhoods. "The absolute amount of interracial neighboring is very low regardless of the neighborhood's racial balance." (Bradburn *et al.*, 1971, p. 165.)

The Reasons for Lack of Contact

The Jewish people offered several explanations for the lack of contact. The simplest one was "we hardly see them." In many cases both husband and wife worked, and some people reported that although they knew they had black neighbors, they had seen them only once or twice. To this some add, especially those living in apartment buildings and having several black neighbors, "We cannot tell one from the other." Most people, however, saw and recognized their black neighbors.

A most common explanation for the lack of any meaningful relations between Jews and blacks was the difference in life cycle stage. Regardless of the racial difference it is important to bear in mind that whereas most Jews in Mattapan were in their sixties or seventies, the blacks were mainly young families with children. The difference in life cycle stage results very often in the lack of common interests. "I hardly see my neighbors. I'm working all day. They have small children. I have very little in common with them." Or, "I say hello and that's it. I have very little in common with them. When my children were small everybody on the street had small children." Gans emphasizes life cycle stage as well as class as the two most important characteristics for understanding the patterns of social life of a community. (Gans, 1968.)

In some rare cases the differences in life cycle stage led to conflict. Some misunderstandings were caused by the mere fact that suddenly there were children around. An elderly woman complained that black children rang her doorbell and ran away, which had never happened before. She related this to the incoming blacks, and tended to forget that until two years before, her apartment building had been occupied exclusively by elderly people. Some complained that "now there are so many kids here and they make a lot of noise." "The Jews were of my age or older and there weren't any children here." "I cannot take a lot of noise, I'm a sick woman."

In the few cases where Jews and blacks were of the same life cycle stage, and the children were of the same age, the Jewish people reported that the children played together. "My son plays with them and they come here." "My daughter plays with their children and they are very nice." Some of those who have teenage children reported that they were friendly with black teenagers in their neighborhood.

In most cases, however, contact between children does not lead to contact between their parents. Some complained that their black neighbors were snobbish, and others felt that the blacks did not want any contact with them. "When my neighbors moved in I brought them a cake, but they don't want anything to do with us. My neighbor is as sour as a cucumber." Another man complained about his black neighbor: "I passed once and wanted to say hello but he turned his head. That was enough for me."

Not everyone generalized about the black neighbors. Some people realized that there are blacks and blacks. "The black neighbors across the street are very friendly. We don't socialize but we talk on the street. They were here and we were there. Those on the other side aren't nice and act as if, 'You don't bother us and we don't bother you.' It seems that most of them don't want anything to do with us, but that's O.K."

Some Examples of Exceptional Relations with Blacks

In some exceptional cases it seems that blacks made a real effort to establish friendly relations with their Jewish neighbors. A woman recalled that the first black who moved onto the street came to her house and introduced herself. An exceptional story was told by an eighty-year-old man, who lived with his slightly younger wife in a one-family house. There were some Jewish families on the block but the majority were black:

> When they first moved in, the black neighbor came in and said we must give them the honor and come to a party where the chaplain is going to *bench* [bless] their house. We went there. The house was full of *schwarze*. We were the only whites. Everyone said my wife is the queen of the street. . . . Then they helped me cut the grass when the gardener stopped coming. I bought them presents for Christmas. After the first snow storm, they came and shoveled the snow—I didn't ask them. Later I gave them a bottle of whiskey.

It is interesting that in the few cases where people reported closer neighborly relations the initiative always came from the black neighbor, as in the following case: "The next-door neighbors are very nice. At the beginning I couldn't tell one from another, they all looked alike to me. She started to say hello to me, and when I was sick, she offered to do the shopping for me. She is a biochemist."

In one or two cases where Jews lived on an almost completely black street of one- and two-family brick houses, the Jews had the feeling of being protected by the blacks. "The people across the street are very nice. He's an engineer and they don't bother us. I put the trash outside and he helped me. They watch the neighborhood."

The fact that Jews were at first apprehensive about the incoming blacks is understandable. Some people admitted that they were nervous before their first black neighbors moved in, but then they realized that the blacks were professionals who kept their property well and sent their children to private schools. In this respect it seems true that attitudes follow behavior and not the other way around. (Pettigrew, 1973.) People simply did not know what to expect in the beginning. "We weren't used to it. We were brought up in a Jewish ghetto and I don't think it was good. Now I am color blind to my neighbors across the street." A mother of a seven-year-old boy remarked that "My son is used to playing with children of all kinds; he plays with blacks and gentiles. For him it won't be any problem to live in an integrated neighborhood. We grew up in a Jewish area; we loved our little ghetto."

Differences in Life Styles

The Mattapan Jews, especially the older ones, have a different life style from that of the blacks. It seems difficult, for instance, for some Jewish people to understand that "the kids are playing outside after dark. When our kids were small they knew that they had to come home when it got dark." Many elderly people do not like "the way they dress and grow their hair." An old man even asked me if "they were born with hair like this?" The blacks' big cars are another theme for disapproval.

Differences in life style are mainly manifested in small things. Some people said, "They don't bother us, but the food they cook smells funny." Some mentioned other subtle differences such as that of language. "There are some idioms we cannot use in front of them. For instance, to say, 'Come here boy,' is very offensive, but with time, this will pass."

A few people assumed that blacks have different values and therefore were reluctant "to start with them." A woman living on a small street where a few black families have started to move in complained about the children on the next street. "On West Seldon Street there are children. They are wild and make a lot of noise. They are wilder than white children, and besides, to a white kid you can say something and if he won't listen, you can go to the parents. But you are afraid to say anything to these kids—you don't know what they are up to."

Others who tried, on the other hand, to communicate with the parents have a different opinion. Many claimed that the black children are very well educated and that their parents discipline them. A Jewish grocer remarked that his black clients told him, "If you have any troubles with my boy, just tell me." Some Jewish people even noticed that black children sometimes helped the Jewish elderly to shovel the snow and did other similar chores, adding, "no Jewish kid will do it." Again we see that change in values follows behavior and does not precede it.

Some Jews believed that the feeling of uneasiness and apprehension was reciprocal, and that the blacks too were nervous about the contact with Jews. One woman commented, "The blacks are very good neighbors, they want to keep it a good street. They want to better themselves. They are educated and their children are more disciplined than the Jewish children. They are friendly on the street, but they don't mix because they don't know how they'd be accepted."

Do Blacks Want the Area to Remain Integrated?

One of the questions with which the Jews were preoccupied is whether the blacks in the area want them to stay or leave. In other words, are the Mattapan blacks interested in having the area remain integrated? Opinions differed on this point.

It is clear to all the Jewish people that the middle class or stable working-class blacks "are running away from their own people" and are very much concerned with preserving the good neighborhood. The Jews noticed that their black neighbors are afraid of the "trash" from Dorchester and Roxbury and are victimized by them not less than they themselves. "The blacks who are living here are suffering from them more than the whites. They give all the blacks a bad name."

The question is only whether the blacks are interested in having Mattapan become a "respectable" black area or if they want it to remain biracial. To some people it seems clear that "the neighbors here don't want it to become an all black ghetto." One man noticed that "when we painted our house, they were afraid we were leaving." A couple living in a two-family house together with their black landlord recalled, "At the beginning we thought they'd want us to leave because they'll probably want to rent to a black couple, but they don't want us to leave. They know that when blacks move here, they'll get many children and a lot of noise. I think he is sorry he bought here. They asked me a few times what happened with the neighborhood like you are asking me now."

Some Jews, however, did feel that the blacks want them to move out of the area. It does not seem surprising that the few Jews who lived in the old apartment buildings which were almost completely black shared this view. "They want the whites out, they don't say it, but that's what they want." A woman living in a three-decker apartment building remarked that her black landlord lived downstairs and "I think they want us out. They always ask questions." What seems surprising is that a few people living in the "good" section expressed the same opinion. "They want to bring their children up in a good way, they are running away from their own kind, but they feel that the neighborhood belongs to them—that we should go someplace else—I feel like an outsider." Another man commented that the blacks, like any other ethnic group, want to live among their own people.

The two men I interviewed who were active in the Mattapan Block Association, an integrated group led by blacks and aimed at stabilizing the neighborhood, claimed that the blacks had stopped inviting them to meetings. The reason, according to one of them, was that "The Association is fighting only for blacks, they are not so much interested in stabilizing the area, as in the fact that blacks aren't able to buy where they want to." Most neighborhood associations are not mixed, the majority being black with one or two white, non-Jewish block associations. Since most of these groups are organized on more or less a street level, it seems clear that on the predominantly black streets they consist mainly of black members. There seems to be one mixed block association on a black-Jewish street.

It is, of course, impossible to know the attitude of the Mattapan blacks toward an integrated area and whether they want the Jews to stay or leave unless somebody interviews them. It would be interesting to know whether the intentions some Jews attribute to the blacks are real or imagined. From the information I gathered it is hard to generalize about whether the black residents want Mattapan to remain an integrated area or not. It seems clear, however, that the main issue for the black people is not whether Mattapan will remain integrated, but rather the quality of the community. They fight to keep Mattapan a clean and safe area with good city services. Pettigrew, in summarizing survey data dealing with blacks' attitudes toward living in integrated neighborhoods, concludes that "When presented a meaningful choice between an all black neighborhood and a mixed neighborhood blacks overwhelmingly favored the latter." (Pettigrew, 1973, p. 43.) There might be a difference, however, between a hypothetical situation such as most survey questions deal with and actually living in an integrated neighborhood.

Since only a few Jews had more than a casual relation with blacks, it was difficult for them to really know the blacks' view on this point. Not surprisingly, those Jews who had more than casual contact with blacks shared the opinion that the latter want the neighborhood to remain integrated. It might be, of course, that blacks disagree on this point as much as Jews do and that those who are seeking contact with their Jewish neighbors are those who want to live in a biracial community.

Previous Contact and Attitudes Toward Blacks

As we have seen, most Mattapan Jews do not mind having black neighbors. "I wouldn't mind blacks on my floor if they are nice." "I don't mind to have black neighbors if they are decent people." "I don't mind to live in an integrated community."

There are, of course, exceptions. Some people reject their black neighbors even if they are "good" blacks. "They don't bother me, I keep to myself, but I don't want to live with them even if they are nice." A woman living on a still all-white street remarked, "I don't want to live with them. I might sound bigoted, but that's the way I feel. Even with the nice ones, after what they did to the whole Jewish people." One extreme opinion was expressed by a man who said, "Blacks are still blacks and it does not matter which class."

Those people although they are a minority, expressed no doubt very strong antiblack feelings. It is impossible to say why some people are more prejudiced than others without going into a psychological analysis. "I hate them because of what they did to the houses of the Jews in Dorchester—look what they did to the synagogues. I don't trust them."

Allport defines prejudice as "a feeling, favorable or unfavorable, toward a person or thing, prior or not based on actual experience." (Allport, 1958, p. 7.) Although it is very hard to judge, it seems that at least part of the people interviewed who expressed antiblack feelings have had bad experiences with blacks in areas other than housing. Our famous cab driver explained his feelings: "I was very bitter against them in the army. Then I decided not to be prejudiced until I got robbed by two *schwarze* in my cab in Roxbury. That turned me very bitter against them." Or a woman reported that "My husband had a meat market in Roxbury, they burned it down and it was not worth fixing it, so he just left and moved. You ask me why I don't like blacks—that's the reason." Some have had bad experiences as employers. "The *Globe* said Jews are racists; they made a racist out of me. I said to myself, 'A man is a man.' I was good to them and they put me out of business." A woman who was beaten up by black youngsters confessed, "We don't know the black people, but when we get to know them it's only for the bad side."

Pettigrew argues that "more interracial contact can lead either to greater prejudice and rejection or to greater respect and acceptance, depending on the situation in which it occurs." (Pettigrew, 1973, p. 60.) The situations described here are definitely not going to lead to greater respect and acceptance. A woman who had a bad experience with blacks admitted, "I didn't hate them until I came here; now I hate them as they hate us." The negative impact of contact has also been found in studies in areas other than housing. (Armor, 1972.) Although positive attitudes toward the blacks might be limited to the specific situation, negative attitudes, as we have seen from the quotes, are generalized from one situation to another.

Not all people who are prejudiced base their antiblack sentiments on personal experience. Sometimes the knowledge of the bad experiences of others is enough to provoke these feelings. "I admit that we are prejudging. It's not because of their color. You hear so much that you don't want to know them closer."

What Is Wrong with Blacks Next Door?

As we have already noted, those people who resented living among blacks, even if they were "nice," were a minority among the Mattapan Jews. Most people interviewed did not mind their black neighbors. Yet, Mattapan is an unstable neighborhood and it is enough to read the popular press to realize that this experiment of integrating the neighborhood has not been too successful.

No one can explain better what has been going wrong than the people themselves:

> I don't mind the black neighbors, but what they bring with them. The moment they move into the area the crime rises, schools are beginning to be bad, property value drops. All of a sudden you get used to seeing black faces. After the first family moves in, you see them driving on your street. They look at you like a fish in a show room. You feel like a prisoner in your own community.

"The trouble is with their friends and relatives." "The people here are O.K. The trouble is with those in the three-deckers. Blacks feel now they can walk more freely in the area, it's open to them and they who don't live here are causing the trouble." To illustrate their point, that is, that they were not against their black neighbors per se, some people mentioned that they had Chinese neighbors and that "They are wonderful people who don't bother anybody and are very quiet."

The main concern of the Mattapan Jews is not the "nice" blacks living next door but the consequences of their entry, that is, that the area becomes "open" to blacks. A drop in property value seems to be one of the biggest concerns of the Mattapan Jews. The academic argument that property value is not supposed to drop, as some studies claim (Millen, 1973), seems irrelevant from the point of view of the people. They believe they are going to lose money and that is what counts for them. "The moment blacks move in it cheapens the street. Whites want to sell. The prices are going down. People are afraid they'll lose money." Therefore, as somebody said, "I don't mind having black neighbors, I resent that the value of my property which I worked hard for will decline." People are convinced that they have already lost money. "Last year I could get $30,000 for the house, now I'm not sure I'll get $20,000. The property value goes down because they don't have so much money to pay for the houses." This fear, real or imagined, poses a great threat to the people. For them buying a house has been a major investment, and it is extremely important to them.

Another consequence of blacks moving into the area is connected with the rising crime rate. As we have seen, crime has indeed risen tremendously in recent years in Mattapan. Most people agreed that their black neighbors were not those who commit the crimes and that they were victimized as much as the white people. (Although the one woman who has been beaten up four times and does not dare to leave her apartment feels safe in the building because she is almost the only white person there.) Most people feel that blacks are not less vulnerable to crime than they themselves. The one man who was invited to the housewarming party of his black neighbor reported, "They broke into my house and into the house of the black neighbor. He said to me, 'When I retire, I'm going back to the South.'"

Yet, in an indirect way people see a relationship between the "nice" black neighbors and the rising crime rate. The moment they moved into the neighborhood, the area became "open" to all blacks. "It isn't those who live here who commit the crimes, but whenever blacks move into the area, other blacks come and walk here more freely. If a black will walk around Brookline or Newton it will look suspicious because no blacks live there." A few times a story of two women being robbed by a black in the lobby of one of the apartment buildings was repeated. The women thought the black man who followed them lived in the same building. Thus, from the point of view of the Mattapan Jews, it seems quite logical to "blame" their black neighbors for the increasing crime.

The biggest problem for the Mattapan Jews seems to be the realization that the moment blacks move into the area, more changes are going to occur. It is clear that people were bothered by this feeling of uncertainty. "The colored people who are here seem to be O.K. We don't know them, both husband and wife work. But who will come, the cheaper class will be after them, that's the way it started in Roxbury and Dorchester." Or another couple whose only black neighbors recently moved onto the street said:

> We have black neighbors, they are probably nice people, but can you tell me it's going to stay like this? Now he has a white tenant, but he'll move out and he'll get only a colored one. So, O.K., he has money and keeps the house nice, but who knows who will be his tenant? Who knows who are his friends? You don't know if they are troublemakers and I don't want to take any chances. It's only the feeling of what's coming next.

Becoming a Minority in the Area

This very real fear of what is coming next is connected with the feeling that the Jews are becoming a minority in the area. This was another cause of anxiety for the Mattapan Jews. Inevitably the Jewish people regarded the blacks as invading "their" neighborhood. "The whole street changed, we don't feel it's our community any more." One woman even suggested that "perhaps people don't like the idea that they are forced to live with blacks. If they could have chosen it, it's something else, but the blacks came into the street without asking them." (This situation is, of course, very different from that in public housing projects where blacks and whites enter simultaneously.)

People had strong feelings of being pushed out of the area and of becoming a minority. "We didn't mind at the beginning when there were a few colored people here. I said, 'Fine, it's an integrated area,' but now there are hardly any whites left." "You see a lot of black children playing around and that's a funny feeling. I feel like a stranger here, we are the odd ones now. I am not prejudiced, I'm just not used to it and feel funny."

The problem of visibility seems to be a crucial one in a mixed area. People feel uncomfortable when they suddenly discover that they are a very visible white minority. "You feel funny when you ride the streetcar and there are only three whites." The Mattapan Jews felt so uncomfortable that they even sympathized with the first blacks moving into an all white area. "I think the first black who moves into a white area must feel terrible. Maybe he thinks that after him others will follow."

The realization that they are "the odds" prevents people from even using some of the neighborhood services. Molotch claims that "fear of exposure and mutual suspiciousness between members of two races inhibit biracial sharing of public places which serve as a loci of private behavior." (Molotch, 1969b, p. 891.) This is definitely true in Mattapan. A woman described a visit to the Chinese restaurant as follows, "The people were nice, all well dressed, but it was funny to be the only whites."

People even feel strange in anonymous public places which do not "serve as a loci of private behavior." Thus, they try to avoid those supermarkets, for instance, which are predominantly black. "I don't like to go to the First National because there might be three white people there and that's a funny feeling. Now we are the odds that everybody is looking at." This is true also for other impersonal services such as transportation. "I don't like to take the bus on Morton Street because I'm the only white person, so I walk to the next stop towards Irish Dorchester, there you'd see fewer blacks." No wonder that people complained "what kind of a community is this when I cannot use the services any more?"

Concern about the Future

It seems clear that what is wrong with the neighborhood is not the black neighbors, but what follows when the area becomes open to blacks. One wonders to what extent the problem of mixed neighborhoods like Mattapan is a racial problem and to what extent it is a class problem. Because, after all, the main fear of people is not of the "nice," "respectable" home owners who live next door but of those who are attracted by them into the area, that is, the "trash" coming after them. This means the second wave of black residents and the walkers and drivers who feel the area is now open to them. This fear seems to be a very real one because it happened before. "I don't mind living among the nice ones, but I don't know who'll come after them like it was in Dorchester." Could anybody assure these people that the poor blacks will not follow and move into the area? And if this is going to happen, not only their common sense but even social science questions the desirability of socioeconomic mixing.

One of the interesting questions at this point is: do the Mattapan blacks share these concerns with the Mattapan Jews? In other words, do they feel the same way toward those who might follow them into the area? It is of course impossible to answer these questions without studying the Mattapan blacks. However, from a few interviews with people who are familiar with the Mattapan blacks and with a few black residents, one gets the impression that they are concerned with keeping the "wrong type of people" out of the area. This means large families, people on welfare, and so forth—black or white, including gypsies. As one black community leader explained while referring to poor blacks: "They are not my kind of people although they are my people."

Like any other home owners the black people are concerned about the value of their property and do not want it to depreciate. (This point has been demonstrated by some black residents who testified at the Senate hearings.) Therefore they are very anxious that the incomers will keep the houses and the area from running down.

Some of the activities of various neighborhood groups which are directed toward keeping Mattapan a good, safe, and clean community could also be interpreted as an effort to keep lower class people out of the area (although not said so). The neighborhood groups tried to convince HUD (and in several cases succeeded) to demolish foreclosured properties which were dangerous instead of reselling or rerenting them. We mentioned earlier the opposition of various groups to more liquor stores and bars in the area, probably because these institutions attract a certain kind of population loitering around them. The street patrols could be regarded as another example of discouraging "the wrong kind of people" to walk and drive around the neighborhood.

The problems middle-class blacks face in preserving their neighborhoods have been reported in other studies. Drake and Cayton (1962) noted that "The 'ambitious' Negroes are unable to keep their communities 'middle-class' because the Black Ghetto is too small to accomodate its population and the less well-to-do must filter into these 'best' areas." (Drake and Cayton, 1962, p. 659.)

Pettigrew argues that "an effective way to alter opposition, white and black, to interracial housing is to have them live successfully in such housing." (Pettigrew, 1973, p. 59.) Following Allport (1958) he refers to four characteristics of the contact situation which are preconditions for successful contact: the two groups should possess equal status, seek common goals, be cooperatively interdependent, have the support of authorities. Most of these characteristics are absent in the encounter of blacks and Jews in Mattapan. It is not clear whether they seek common goals, and they are not cooperatively dependent on each other with the support of authorities. This, however, does not seem to be the main problem. Even those Jews who established some meaningful relations with their black neighbors shared the same concerns as the other Jews. A neighborhood is not a closed social entity, and people are exposed to many other factors which have nothing to do with their next door neighbors; "you don't live only on the street, you live in an area."

Most studies agree that many factors are involved in housing choice, and attitudes toward blacks are only one of them. Bradburn even claims that "it seems reasonable to conclude from these facts that behavior, at least as residential choice is concerned, is relatively independent of attitudes." (Bradburn, *et al.*, 1969, p. 124.) Pettigrew wonders why attitudes toward desegregation in housing changed favorably in spite of the fact that urban neighborhoods have not become less segregated. He suggests that since housing is not a closed system, attitudes toward desegregation in this area have been affected by factors outside the housing market.

This is probably true, but there might be an additional reason. If a few years ago (and I suspect that even today), the Mattapan Jews had been asked a question similar to that NORC usually asks, "If a Negro, with just as much education and income as you have, moves into your block, would it make a difference to you?" most of them would have answered sincerely, "No." And indeed, if a few "nice," "respectable" blacks would move into their neighborhood, without all the other changes occurring, most people would not mind because "It's not the blacks that live here, they are different from all others." It is not, as we have seen, the black neighbors which cause the anxiety, it is what comes along with them: "That it's not the neighbors, it's the neighborhood that drives us out."

CHAPTER SEVEN

Prospects for the Future

Up to this point we have described what it is like to live in a
changing neighborhood. One of the questions we tried to answer
was why the Mattapan Jews are still living in the area. As we have
seen, despite the fact that they had not yet moved, the remaining
people were very concerned about forthcoming changes. In this
chapter we will discuss the future plans of the Mattapan Jews. We
will also examine how they perceive the future of the area and
will try to understand why Mattapan could not become an integrated neighborhood.

The Decision-Making Process

The Mattapan Jews can be divided into three groups regarding their plans for the future. A small minority have decided to

remain in the area, no matter what further changes occur. About a third of the people have already made up their minds and have decided to move out of the area. Over half of the Mattapan Jews still hesitate and do not have immediate plans for leaving the neighborhood.

The Immobile People

Not surprisingly, only a small minority of people claimed that they do not intend to move to another area. Most of them are people over seventy who simply feel they cannot change their place of residence any more. "I know the whole street is going to become black because people are selling, but I'm going to stay no matter what happens. I'm too old to move, we are almost eighty years old and we are going to die here." A seventy-year-old renter claimed, "We moved five times in the last ten years. We are too old to move any more." Another lonely old woman put it this way: "I'm stuck. There is nowhere to go." Personal problems are another reason for staying in the area. A woman who has a retarded son does not want to move because she lives close to the synagogue, the only place her son goes regularly.

Eight out of those who claimed they will not move in any case are home owners. Besides the fact that they feel they are too old to move, they are very attached to their houses and love them. "I don't want to move. I like my house; it's big and convenient. I don't want to go to an apartment building. We finished paying the mortgage, and now if I move, I'll have to pay high rent. I don't want to lose all I invested in the house."

All those who are definite in their intentions to stay live either on streets which are completely black or on those which are in the process of change. Some feel, or rather hope, that these locations are not going to change any more, that their streets have stabilized. "I think that the worst is over. I think that the area quieted down. Those who are here are not going to sell; I think it's going to stay like this." In the very few cases where Jews are surrounded by black home owners, that might be more than wishful thinking. A few play with the illusion that "people here don't want to sell. We talk about it with the neighbors. If nobody sells the place will be as it is now." Nevertheless, the main reason for staying in the area is not because of this optimistic view of the future but rather that people feel they are too old to move, that they are trapped. "There is no place to go."

Most Jews are going to move out of Mattapan sooner or later. Some have already decided to move and have made plans for the future in other areas. Others are still waiting to see what happens. But even the hesitants admitted that "eventually we'd have to move because the area will get more and more black and I don't want to be the only white person on the street."

The Movers—What Made Them Decide?

Twenty-nine people were in the process of moving during the period of the interviews, that is, they were trying to sell their houses or were looking for new ones or for apartments. One of the interesting questions is what gave those people the final push to decide that they had to get out of the area. We have seen already why those who are still in Mattapan have not yet moved. So, after staying for such a long period in the changing neighborhood, what made them finally decide to move now?

The reasons are many. "A year ago we decided we had it. I don't know why, but we decided we had it." "We decided it's time to move. I don't know what made us decide, but I feel as an outsider. It's a funny feeling that I don't belong here any more." Other people were able to point to more specific factors which gave them the last push. Some people played with the idea of moving for a while, not knowing whether to move or not. "But now since colored people moved into the street, we decided to sell." Most of the movers did not decide when the first blacks moved onto their street but rather when they realized that most white people were moving out. "We decided to sell when the two neighbors across the street sold. Now the street is almost completely black."

For some people the decision to move was connected with bad personal experiences. "The neighbors downstairs were robbed. We came into the house just when the two black guys came out of the apartment. One of them tried to grab me. They didn't do anything to me, but we decided to leave. Till then we thought about it, but didn't actually decide it." One woman living on an almost completely black street plainly said: "I want to get out of here. I'm scared with all the black people around." The sudden realization that she was living in a "bad" area gave another woman the last push. "Two years ago my house was robbed. The policeman said the insurance will pay the damage, but won't give me a new insurance because it's a high risk area. To know you are living in a high risk area isn't very pleasant. At that time I decided to sell and put my house on the market."

Selling a House in Mattapan. Eleven home owners put their houses "on the market." For home owners it is not easy to sell a house in Mattapan, and most of them complained about it. "We put our house for sale but nobody came to look at it. Ours is hard to sell because it is a small house (five rooms) and they usually have big families. They could get now all the houses they want with the mortgages they get."

At that time the FHA was giving mortgages less easily than before, and that of course made it harder for people to sell.

> Last July I decided to put my house for sale. I went to the FHA and they appraised it for $26,500. I had to pay $40 for the appraisal. Why do I have to pay two points and they pay only one point to the FHA? I just decided to sell when the FHA didn't give any mortgages, but you cannot sell here without the FHA. I had a buyer in February, but she didn't have the $2,500 the FHA asked for deposit. So in April she said she cannot buy and I gave her back the money. They are checking if the person can afford to buy a house, because in many cases they just couldn't. I hope to find another customer.

The main concern of those who decided to sell is that they may lose money. "We asked for $25,000 but I'm not sure we'd get

$20,000." Or, "We paid five years ago $20,000 and put into the house $3,000. I hope to get it out but it's hard to sell now." In general people have the feeling that they have already lost money. "The house is two years 'for sale,' but we cannot get the price we asked. The FHA appraised it for $33,000 [a duplex], and we asked $31,000, and we don't want to go down. Five years ago we could have gotten $40,000, but we didn't want to sell then." The general assumption is that "all property went up except in Mattapan." For the Mattapan Jews the loss of money because of declining property value, at least as they see it, is a very real problem.

About half of those who decided to sell have already bought another house in a different area. "We put our house for sale and bought a new one in Randolph. It's beyond our means but we have no other choice." Some realize they will have to pay a high price for moving to another area. As a middle-aged woman put it: "We are moving to Randolph. We won't be able to send our kids to college, but there is no other choice if they want a roof over their heads." The others who have not bought a home claim they do not know where their new home will be. "I don't know where to go; I'm forced to move."

Most of those who are trying to sell live in what was once the Jewish section of Mattapan which is in the process of change. Only two live in the predominantly non-Jewish section, which is to a large extent still white. They feel rather uncomfortable about selling to blacks. "We said we'd only sell to whites, but the broker said if he puts it in the paper he has to sell to anyone. I'd feel bad for my tenants to sell it to a black. I'll do so only if others do it too." Another woman living on a mixed street confessed, "I wanted to sell two years ago but my husband didn't let me. He didn't want to be the first one to sell to blacks. Now that so many on the street sold, we also did the move."

The Renters. Eighteen renters also decided to move (in addition to the owners). The relatively larger number of renters deciding to leave is interesting, for it has been assumed that it is easier to achieve stable racial mixing in rental houses than in owner-occupied ones. (Wolf and Lebeaux, 1969; Millen, 1973.) It is true that renters moved into Mattapan at a time when hardly any Jews had bought houses in the area. In the long run, however, when the area has already changed a great deal, renters are no less eager to move out than owners. Some of the eighteen renters who want to move out live in the three-deckers in the "bad" area, but they are only a small share of the number. Among those renters who decided to leave are a few who live in one of the apartment building complexes. They suddenly discovered that "the rent is too high for this area." In one other case a woman living in a predominantly white section admitted, "The main reason we want to leave is because of the apartment." Yet, most renters who decided to move did so because they wanted to get out of the neighborhood.

It would seem easier for renters than for owners to move from one apartment to another, but many of them cannot afford simply to get up and leave. "We really don't know where to go. We could not afford to pay high rent." Some try to get into a middle-income housing project, but the waiting list is long. "We applied for housing in Cummings Tower—it's subsidized, but nobody moves out. We have to wait until somebody dies."

Some found their new apartment through the help of the Jewish organizations. "First we looked ourselves, but rents are so expensive. Then we went to the CJP. They found us an apartment in Brockton. It's a middle-income housing development. There will be also non-Jews there, but at least there will be many Jews." Others found their apartments through relatives.

Their New Places. The general trend is for the Mattapan Jews to move southward to the South Shore. Often people would comment that "Randolph is almost like Blue Hill Avenue." Interestingly, the Mattapan Jews are moving to these areas even though they are aware that blacks are coming to the same places. "There are blacks in Randolph, but they are of another kind. If they can afford such a house, and they do not get the FHA mortgages there, they must be of a better kind." Or, "Those blacks are real professional, otherwise they couldn't afford a

$50,000 house." People realized that "in Milton there are also blacks, but not as much as here." The same logic also applied to renters. "We don't mind some blacks, but I don't want to be a minority. The colored people in Brockton can at least pay $165 per month. The Housing Authority screens them."

Strangely, these people were not talking about "the trash coming after them." Only a few are afraid of the repeated experience and prefer a mixed neighborhood to a Jewish one. An old man observed sadly that the only place for those Jews to run to will be the ocean.

Not all of those who are moving are happy about it. When they compare the costs and benefits of leaving, they themselves cannot decide whether the move is for the better or not. One woman described it this way:

> We applied for the Housing Project in Brockton. Frankly, I don't like it there. Here I have three bedrooms and there I'll have only two. Here I have a porch. You don't know who your neighbors are going to be; in the low income project they have to accept everybody. Here it's very handy; there the stores are one mile away. But what can I do? We want to get out of here.

Those people who decided to move, owners and renters, who find it difficult to carry out their decision because they have not found a new home yet, seem to be very preoccupied by the idea of moving. "It's always on my mind." "I think of it day and night; I go to bed with it."

The Hesitants—What Will Make Them Move?

About half of the Mattapan Jews do not have immediate plans to move out of the area but realize, on the other hand, that sooner or later they are going to leave. The hesitants can be divided into two groups: those who live in what is called "still a good area" and do not feel an immediate pressure to leave, and those who for various personal reasons stay for a while in the neighborhood, whether owning or renting.

The Owners. Most owners, although not all of them, who delay their decision for other than personal reasons, live on a

more or less all-white or predominantly white street. Their decision will depend to a large extent on the future changes. "If it
stays like this, it's fine. I only don't want to be left the only white
on the street as I was in Dorchester." Past experience is an
important comparative point; people do not want to repeat it. "I
don't intend to sell as long as nothing happens here. The
moment it gets bad on the Hill, I'll have to move."

Most people claimed they will stay "as long as I can." Naturally, for different people different situations indicate that they
cannot stay in the area any more. Thus, "as long as I can" means
"as long as nothing happens to me," "as long as the neighbor next
to us stays," "as long as they don't bother me," or, "when it gets to
the point that I can't sleep at night, when the street becomes dirty."

The main fear, however, is that the streets will become all
black. The speculation about whether this is going to happen
preoccupies people's minds. The "ifs" are so many that people do
not know what is going to happen. A woman living on a still all-
white street summarized it this way:

> I don't mind black neighbors if they are decent people. I only
> don't want to be the only white one on the street. I really don't
> know what will happen with the street. There is one house for
> sale and I don't think a white person will buy here. Jews
> definitely won't buy here. They like to better themselves and
> that's not considered a good neighborhood any more. I
> wouldn't buy here now although I like it very much.

On those streets which do not yet have any blacks there is
always the speculation of who is going to be the first to sell to
blacks—who will be the gatekeeper? "People always sell and buy
for different reasons. They don't want to do it to their neighbors."
Yet, there is always the fear that in the end people will have no
choice but to sell to blacks because at this stage of change whites
are not going to buy in Mattapan. Although there have been a
few cases where white people have bought homes on these
streets, they are regarded as exceptions. "I don't know why the
white girl bought here; I wouldn't buy a house here now." The
feeling of uncertainty came out over and over again during

interviews with the people living in the "good" section. "This area is still good, but I don't know for how long. They are coming in here; you see them on the side streets. The trouble is you never know if whites are going to buy here. Most of the people are elderly without children. The first black who moves in, that's the end of the street." Most people do not think, however, that the first black is the "end of the street." As we have seen, what bothers people is what will happen after the first blacks move in.

As we have seen, most people realized that "their" neighborhood was changing only when looking out their windows they saw a black face. It seems, however, that at that stage of change, most people realized even without actually seeing it, that their street was going to become black.

Not all of the people who decided to wait and see what happened were without black neighbors. As a matter of fact, most of these people lived on streets where there were some black people and they did not seem to mind it. "As it is now, it's really fine. We, the whites, are those who make the change. If it stays like this, it's O.K., but you don't know. In Dorchester it took only six months until the whole street changed." The fear of remaining the "only white" does not sound so unrealistic when one keeps in mind that some of the people have already gone through the experience of living in a changing neighborhood.

Some of those who decided to wait and see live in great anxiety. "We live from day to day." A few people reported they had not done anything to their houses, although they needed repairs, because they did not know what the future would be like. Yet, on the other hand, the fact that some houses on the street are in bad condition serves as a warning sign to others:

> This street is nice and clean and we want it this way. But the two houses on our side are for sale. They are very old and in very bad condition and they won't get a good price for them, so the cheaper class will buy them. We really don't want to move, but I don't want to be the only white person. I don't want to leave, but I have the feeling we'll have to.

As we have seen, most of those who decided to wait and see live in the section which is still "good." Some, however, live on streets which are undergoing rapid change, and some have already changed. Those staying in Mattapan for the time being remain mainly because of various personal reasons. "We don't intend to sell now; we have to stay in the city; maybe in two years when we retire." Some are waiting until their children finish high school and do not want to move now to an area farther away from the school. There are various other personal reasons such as: "I feel now I have nothing to look for here. So I figure in a year when my older son moves out of the house and only the little one will be with me, we'll move to an apartment." A few have thoughts of moving to Florida after retirement.

For those who are not in the process of selling yet, the question of losing money is not as acute as for those who have put their houses up for sale. Since the former have not tried to sell, they do not know for sure whether they are going to lose money. In general, people agree that property value drops the moment blacks move in. They themselves are not sure, however, if they have already lost money. Thus, a woman living on an all-white street commented, "Until now I don't think we lost on the house because we bought it very cheap, but I'm sure we'll lose after the first black moves into the street." On the other hand, a man living on a street that is already beyond the first stage of panic selling argued, "I think that if I wait and not sell in panic, I'll get more. Those who sold in panic set the low price. I decided not to sell in panic." A few made the calculation that as the rent they would have to pay for an apartment would always be higher than their mortgage, "even if we lose two or three thousand dollars, I'm sure we saved it by staying here."

The Renters. The renters who decided to wait and see what happened seemed to be somewhat less disturbed by the changing neighborhood than the owners. At least they feel they have nothing to lose by waiting. Thus a couple who moved to one of the apartment-building complexes two years ago remarked, "We thought we'd have at least five years here and if we don't like it here we'll move." Some hope that their building will not change too much. "I don't know what will happen with this place. I don't think many colored people can afford to move into these buildings." On the other hand, one of the apartment complexes which had had no blacks was sold, and some of the people interviewed seemed nervous regarding the possibility that the place might open up for blacks.

Some renters who live in the predominantly non-Jewish section still hope that there will be no changes in the near future. "This area might stay for some time white because gentiles live here." Or a woman living in a two-family house together with her gentile landlady hopes that "I'll stay as long as I can; I mean as long as my landlady stays. She does not intend to sell." But even the most optimistic renters agree that "you cannot know if whites won't sell at one end."

Some renters stay in the area temporarily for the same reasons that keep owners in Mattapan for the time being. A widow explained her reason for staying as, "Maybe I'll move to Florida—I have to until my husband's will is carried out."

What Prevents Mattapan from Becoming an Integrated Neighborhood?

No doubt, as some studies have indicated (Millen, 1973; Molotch, 1968), one of the reasons that neighborhoods are segregated is that blacks do not have a free choice of housing. Thus, opening an area to blacks would contribute to residential desegregation. However, neighborhoods might become segregated as well if they are opened only to blacks. The FHA mortgages were given only to black people in order to encourage them to buy homes in the area. These mortgages were denied, deliberately or not, to whites. The effect of this has been, as in the case of the Lewenberg Junior High School, that the area has been changing from white to black.

The section where most of the remaining Mattapan Jews are living is outside the "red line" and is still partly white, but the damage has already been done. Despite the fact that the FHA does not give mortgages as easily as it used to, about 400 buildings have been sold in Mattapan during 1972, the large majority of them outside the "red line."

The way people behave and calculate their steps seems logical and rational from their point of view. People are always selling and buying, especially on those streets where most are elderly people. Whites do not buy in this area any more. Even if the Jewish people have noticed some whites moving in recently, they are regarded as exceptions because the Jews themselves admit that they would not buy in Mattapan today. If no white people are willing to buy in the area, the area will eventually become black. At this stage even the most optimistic people are afraid that in the end they will have to move because they do not want to remain "the only white person on the street."

Although there is no consistent evidence as to when the "tipping point" of a neighborhood occurs (Millen, 1973), it seems clear that Mattapan is already beyond this point. It is interesting to note that although Bradburn *et al.* (1971) found a substantial number of integrated neighborhoods, only a fifth of them had more than 10% blacks.

It was not enough for Mattapan to become an integrated neighborhood by convincing people not to panic and sell (as the Mattapan Organization tried to do). Maybe a better policy would have been to try to attract white people to the area. Wolf and Lebeaux noticed that

Even when efforts to prevent mass flights are successful, when the white residents in those areas grow older and their children leave home, when the spouse dies or when the family leaves the city, these houses will be put on the market. Large numbers of new white buyers must come into these established areas if the areas are to remain mixed. (Wolf and Lebeaux, 1969, p. 502.)

The Mattapan people are, of course, aware of the fact that the area was opened only to blacks. "I would like to see some white families coming in, but I know it won't happen." "The banks should have given these mortgages to anybody. There are enough poor Italians and other people who would have liked to buy a house here if they could." Of course, the belief that "all houses are on sale" and that no whites are going to buy in the area and, therefore, the area will inevitably become all black hastens the process of change and operates as a "self-fulfilling prophecy." (Wolf, 1957.)

The Mattapan Jews are uncertain about whether the blacks want the area to remain biracial or not. In any case their suspicion that blacks are "taking over" accelerates this process of change. The more Jews move out and blacks move in, the stronger the feeling that "It's not our community any more." At this stage one can only agree with the Mattapan Jews who feel that "in five years Mattapan is going to be all black."

CHAPTER EIGHT

Conclusions

The objective of this study has been to describe and analyze a changing neighborhood from the point of view of that segment of the population that remained in the area. The question we were dealing with was how the Jews of Mattapan perceive and interpret the changes in their neighborhood and how they react to them. While summarizing our findings, one should keep in mind that they are limited to one group; we do not know how the Irish and Italian Catholics or the black people perceive the changes in the area.

It is difficult to conclude whether the situation in Mattapan as perceived and described by the remaining Jews is typical of a changing neighborhood. In other words, does it reflect the common experience of people living in a transitional area? Without comparative studies of other neighborhoods and of other groups it would be impossible to draw any broad conclusions from this one case study.

Mattapan is in many respects similar to changing neighborhoods reported in the various case studies mentioned earlier. Like many transitional areas, Mattapan lies on the border of the existing black community. The growth of the black population in Boston, and the displacement of many people because of urban renewal in central-city neighborhoods, inevitably resulted in the expansion of the black community. In addition, many blacks were particularly attracted to Mattapan by the availability of good, reasonably priced housing stock. Finally, the age structure, with its relatively high proportion of elderly people, was typical of that of a transitional neighborhood.

The Unlivable Neighborhood

As noted in the beginning of this study, Mattapan changed rapidly over a period of four years, and its Jewish population declined markedly. The remaining Jews lived through this period; they saw and felt the neighborhood changing. What is an unstable neighborhood like? What does it mean to live in such an area? If our findings have any relevance to changing neighborhoods in general, it is that one can say the changing neighborhood has become an unlivable neighborhood for those who have remained.

The most striking feature of a changing neighborhood is the feeling that one is living in an area which is no longer safe. People are afraid to walk on the streets, and whenever they do go out, they feel they must protect themselves in various ways. In their homes they lock themselves beyond closed doors, and every stranger is regarded as a potential danger. Some do not feel safe any more even in their own homes, and for them the area is indeed a "defeated neighborhood." (Suttles, 1972.) The feeling that "we live in fear" seems to dominate the lives of the Mattapan

Jews to a large extent. They have learned to cope with the situation and adjust to it in various ways: those who hesitate to leave their homes arrange that goods be delivered to them, some are picked up for their shopping, and others have "signals" with service people and with others. Those who still go out try to protect themselves in various ways, such as hiding their money in their shoes. From such behavior it is clear that the area has become unlivable for many of the Mattapan Jews.

How Does a Neighborhood Become Unlivable?

The kind of neighborhood Mattapan is today is not unique. Neighborhoods similar to this, which Suttles (1972) named "defended neighborhoods," have been studied since sociologists first became interested in the urban phenomenon.[1] Traditionally, however, these have been inner-city neighborhoods and not semi-suburban areas such as Mattapan. From the point of view of a neighborhood study, the important question is not so much what is an unlivable neighborhood like, but rather, how and when does an area reach such a point? How and why does it become unlivable?

From all that we can learn from the popular press and from people's recollections, Mattapan had remained a peaceful area up to several years before this study was made. Yet, at one point or another the transformation occurred, and it became an unlivable neighborhood. What happened then to cause people to feel uncomfortable in their neighborhood and to claim that "you are afraid of your own shadow"?

In order to answer this question and to understand the process of neighborhood transformation, it seems necessary to study such an area over a long period of time. Since we studied the Mattapan Jews at only one point in time and did not follow the transition process of the area, it is impossible from our data to answer the question of when and why Mattapan became an unlivable neighborhood. Nevertheless, from the information we collected from the Mattapan Jews, we *can* point to several factors which contributed to this process.

First, it seems that the feeling of discomfort and uneasiness is to some extent inherent in the process of rapid residential change. As we have seen, people are constantly moving out, and, once a street has begun changing, more changes are expected. What seems to bother most people is that the familiar faces disappear and that "in a very short period of time everybody I knew on the street was gone." People suddenly realize that they do not belong to the area any more, that those people who crossed their path every day are moving. As a result of the out-migration of their Jewish neighbors, they find themselves in an unfamiliar and new situation. It is worth noting that most so-called "defended neighborhoods" studied intensively by the Chicago School were unstable areas characterized by a high rate of residential turnover. To illustrate this point of the impact of change and instability, it is useful to compare the people who live on streets which have been changing with those who live on streets which have not yet changed. People living on the latter streets seem to be much less on guard in their daily movements.

Second, the rise in crime rate adds to the feeling that the area has become unlivable. To a large extent the feeling of discomfort is focused around the fear of crime. Crime, according to people's recollections and to the popular press, is a fairly recent phenomenon in Mattapan. It is impossible to record why crime suddenly became such a widespread phenomenon, but from the people's point of view, this is one of the components of the unlivable neighborhood. A large proportion of the population are elderly people and therefore more vulnerable. Many people have been victimized: some have suffered only from property loss, but others have been physically injured. Such personal experience is of course one major source of anxiety, as some people observed, "When you feel it on your skin, you get scared!"

Personal experience, however, is not the only source of

anxiety. The feelings of the Mattapan Jews that the area is not safe any more are often based on the experiences of others and on what the people themselves see, read and hear. The feeling that the neighborhood is no longer safe depends to a large extent on crime on one's street or block group. The point of reference for safety is thus what happens in the very immediate vicinity. One of the important criteria of a "good" street, which one can still walk on without being constantly on guard, is the lack of crime. As we have seen, the "good" streets compared to the "bad" ones are those which have not yet changed much. While it was impossible to compare the different crime rates on different streets in Mattapan, from the subjective point of view of the people, the rise in crime seems to be related to the process of change.

The third important factor contributing to the feeling that Mattapan is an unlivable neighborhood is public opinion and the press. Mattapan is labeled as a "bad" neighborhood, and people suddenly realize they are living in a dangerous area, in a "combat zone." The public image of the neighborhood is related, of course, to the racial change and to the crime rate. Yet, Mattapan became a focus of public attention in 1969 when the area had only begun changing and the crime rate was not yet so high. To a large extent it seems that public opinion shaped the image of Mattapan as a bad and dangerous area which was "going down." This image is shared by the media, by the police, by the insurance agencies, by friends and relatives. No wonder it has an impact on the Mattapan residents themselves. The fact that friends and relatives often refuse to visit indicates to the residents that they live in an area that is no longer desirable. This public image of the area adds, of course, to the anxiety of the Mattapan Jews and has an impact on their behavior. Since the area is labeled as dangerous, people are expected to be careful and to protect themselves and their homes in various ways.

Outside and inside views, however, are not always totally congruent. The public image of Mattapan seems to be based to a large extent on the highly visible changes in the commercial area along Blue Hill Avenue, whereas the inside image is based mainly on changes in an immediate vicinity. For outsiders Mattapan is one undifferentiated area; for the residents, the area is divided into "good" and "bad" sections. The cognitive map, as Suttles (1972) noticed, does not always correspond to the actual physical structure. Nevertheless, "These cognitive maps are part of the social control apparatus of urban areas and are of special importance in regulating spatial movements to avoid conflict between groups" (p. 22). As we have seen, people clearly distinguish between safe and unsafe streets, and behave accordingly.

This brings us to the question of whether it is useful to talk of a changing neighborhood as a whole territorial unit. Mattapan did not change overnight; it changed gradually, street after street, and with a definite pattern going from north to south. As we have seen, the Mattapan Jews did not expect *their* neighborhood to change, and most were caught by surprise when the change did occur. Even people's past experience of living in a changing neighborhood and the fact that adjacent streets were already changing did not serve as a warning sign. Not until black people moved into the Jews' immediate vicinity—so that they could literally see them out of their windows—did they realize that *their* area was changing. Only at that point did the people interviewed believe that change was inevitable. In this respect Mattapan was different from other changing neighborhoods in which people expected the areas to change after the first few black families moved in and made their decision to move accordingly. (Mayer, 1960; Rapkin and Grigsby, 1960; Wolf and Lebeaux, 1969.) Yet, as Schelling rightly noticed, "If tipping occurs primarily because people believe that it does, the relevant definition of the neighborhood will be the one they give it in their hypothesis about tipping." (1972, p. 176.) For the Mattapan Jews, the close territorial unit, that is, the street or block group, was the relevant unit and not the neighborhood at large.

The Unlivable Neighborhood and the Incoming Black People

The most obvious aspect of a racially changing neighborhood is the population change from white to black. To what extent is the feeling that the neighborhood is no longer livable related to the fact that black people are moving in? The Mattapan Jews suddenly see black faces around, and since they are not used to it, they are uncomfortable. The Jews feel they are becoming more and more a visible white minority in the neighborhood. They suddenly realize that they are "the odds" in the area and that Mattapan is not "our community any more."

The black neighbors, however, are not the main cause for concern. The black homeowners are regarded as "respectable" and "nice" people. The fact that they could afford to buy a house and to keep it up properly is for the Mattapan Jews an indication of their status and credibility. The people interviewed very clearly distinguish between their black neighbors and the "cheaper class" living in the three-decker houses. Most Jews said they do not mind having black neighbors. What they do mind, and are very fearful of, is becoming the "only white" on the street. As we have seen, many studies indicate that the fear of becoming a white minority is one of the reasons why people decide to move out of mixed areas. (Wolf and Lebeaux, 1969.) Yet, in contrast to other studies in which this suspicion was based on expectations about the future, in the case of the Mattapan Jews it is very often based on reality. As we have seen, only when their street started changing and black people moved onto it, did most people become aware that "their" neighborhood was changing. As Molotch noticed in the South Shore area in Chicago, the main objection of people is not to the presence of blacks per se, but to the fact that they will be outnumbered by blacks. (Molotch, 1972.) The black neighbors serve in many cases as a warning signal for what is going to come. Once black people started moving onto their streets, the Mattapan Jews were concerned with the future. Yet, it is not blacks living next door that bothers them but the consequences of their entry—"what they bring with them."

Studies dealing with interracial housing stress the point of positive interdependence and contact as a precondition for successful integration. (Pettigrew, 1973.) As we have seen, there is little contact between the Jewish people and their black neighbors, not to speak of closer primary relations. The two groups are of different life cycle stages and apparently have different life styles, therefore seeming to share little in common. Yet, that lack of contact between the two groups does not seem to be the main source of concern, for most people did not have close relations with their Jewish neighbors either. Since the feeling of discomfort is caused mainly by changes in the neighborhood at large and not by the next-door neighbors, lack of close contact with their neighbors does not seem to bother the Mattapan Jews. Thus, although the next-door black neighbors are the strongest indication of change, they themselves are not the main source of concern and anxiety.

What makes the neighborhood unlivable for the Mattapan Jews seems to be related to the fact that the area as a whole has become "open" to blacks in general, that various walkers and drivers feel free to move around, and the Jews feel that the social order in the neighborhood has been disrupted. As Goffman defines it, social order involves the "variously motivated and variously functioning patterns of actual behavior, . . . [and the] routines associated with general rules." (1971, p. x.) The norms and rules of behavior in public areas have been, at least according to the Mattapan Jews, broken down. There seems to be very little open conflict between the two groups. Since the Jews have the feeling of being out of place, they try to avoid as much as possible any contact with the black people. They try to avoid those public places where the majority of users are black, such as certain supermarkets and even some bus lines. It seems, therefore, that although blacks and Jews live close to one another, actual contact between the two groups, even on an instrumental nonpersonal level, is very limited.

Nevertheless, since there is no territorial segregation, especially not in the commercial area, blacks and Jews cannot avoid running into one another. Suttles noticed rightly that "among the available mechanisms, a set of rules governing and restricting spatial movements seem a likely and highly effective means of preserving order." (1972, p. 31.) The Mattapan Jews often perceive the blacks as breaking the rules of behavior in public places. "They don't give you the courtesy of the road." The realization that the social order in the area has been disrupted is threatening for the Mattapan Jews. They feel disturbed by black people who break the rule of "civil inattention" (Goffman, 1963, p. 88); one of the most common complaints of the Mattapan Jews was "the way they look at you." The fact that the social order has been broken down, at least in the eyes of the Jews, is one major reason the neighborhood seems unlivable to them.

The fact that there is no territorial segregation between blacks and Jews makes it harder to distinguish between "good" and "bad" blacks. Since black people are now living in the area, they are no longer noticed, and policing becomes more difficult. Because the Jews are unable to distinguish between the "good" and "bad" blacks, every black encountered becomes a potential danger. The general image of the blacks as violent and aggressive adds to the feeling of anxiety and fear.

We studied and were able to describe the reaction of only one group in Mattapan—the Jewish people—to the process of racial transition. A relevant question would be to what extent does the black home owner share this feeling that the area has become unlivable? In other words, is the feeling of anxiety and discomfort unique to those who remain in a changing area or is it common to all segments of the population? From our data, of course, it is impossible to answer this question, yet it is essential in order to get the whole picture of life in a transitional area. Hearing the stories of Jewish tenants describing the safety devices their black landlords have installed in their houses, learning about the street patrols, and seeing the "Beware of Dog" signs on black homes, one can guess that the feeling of insecurity is, at least to some extent, mutual.

The Significance of the Neighborhood for the Mattapan Jews

The neighborhood concept is not without ambiguity, and much has been written on this subject since Wirth (1938) first described the disappearance of the neighborhood as one of the features of urban life.[2] One of the questions often asked is whether a neighborhood in a big city has any social meaning beyond being just a territorial unit. Various studies, especially in working-class neighborhoods, have indicated that the residential area is still a meaningful social unit. Social ties in an area have been found to be a major source of residential satisfaction. In many cases these cohesive neighborhoods were also ethnic neighborhoods. (Glazer and Moynihan, 1970; Gans, 1962; Whyte, 1943.)

One of the reasons the Mattapan Jews feel insecure and isolated is the disappearance of the Jewish neighborhood, for many people chose their home in Mattapan specifically because it was a Jewish neighborhood. Most of them have lived all their lives in a Jewish area and felt it the most "natural" thing for them to do. Some moved into the area in spite of the conviction that "blacks follow the Jews" and not any other ethnic group. It was important for them to live in a Jewish neighborhood for several reasons. It was important for parents because they wanted their children to associate with other Jewish children and to participate in Jewish institutions. Even for others it was also important, for they wanted to live close to Jewish institutions such as the synagogue and the butcher, and, above all, they wanted to live among Jewish people "of their own kind."

The desire to live in an ethnic neighborhood is not unique among the Mattapan Jews. The important question is, however, what did this ethnic neighborhood mean to the Mattapan people, and why was it so important for them to live in a Jewish area? The Mattapan Jews wanted to live among Jewish people, although they very seldom associated with their Jewish neighbors. As we have seen, Mattapan was far from being an "urban village," typical of many other ethnic neighborhoods. Most people did not have close friends in the area and did not socialize with their neighbors. From what one can learn, it seems clear that Mattapan has never been a close-knit neighborhood. The Mattapan Jews wanted to be close to a kosher butcher, although many of them seldom used his services. They wanted to have a synagogue in their neighborhood in spite of the fact that most people visited it only once a year on the high holidays. Yet, even those people who never visited the synagogue and never used the kosher butcher, noticed when they closed. It was for them an indication that the Jewish neighborhood was gone and that they did not belong to the area any more.

Mattapan had an identity as a Jewish neighborhood, although only slightly over half of the population was Jewish. (The same was true for the West End, which in spite of the fact that the Italians constituted only 42% of the population, was known as an Italian neighborhood.) Jews from all over came to shop on Thursday nights in the area because it was known as a Jewish neighborhood. The synagogue and the butcher and, of course, the other Jewish people symbolized for the Mattapan Jews the fact that it was a Jewish neighborhood. They did not have to socialize with their Jewish neighbors or use the local services; it was enough that they knew they were there. In a way these institutions fulfilled a symbolic function similar to that of the skyline of New York City, as Strauss observed it. "For the purpose served by the symbol, however, it is not really necessary literally to see the view itself—the important thing is to be able to understand what it represented." (Strauss, 1961, p. 11.) For the Mattapan Jews the institutions, services, and the other Jews represented the Jewish identity in the area. In this context one can understand what people meant by saying, "Jews want to be close to a *shul* [synagogue] even if they don't use it." The closing of the Jewish institutions and the out-migration of Jewish neighbors had a strong impact on the Mattapan Jews not because they lost close friends or were suddenly deprived of vital services but because this was an indication that Mattapan had ceased to be a Jewish neighborhood.

Suttles (1972) argues that social ties are not the only basis for residential cohesiveness and suggests territoriality as an alternative explanation for neighborhood solidarity. In a way this was true in Mattapan. As we have seen, although most people did not know their neighbors intimately, they knew their faces and recognized them. Yet, this was only partly true. People not only recognized their neighbors because they crossed one another's paths, but they also knew that they were of their own kind—that they were Jewish. If these findings have any broader implications, one could hypothesize that there are additional bases for neighborhood solidarity than social ties or territoriality. Strong attachment to an area can be based on a common identity or on some other symbolic values. The impact of values on land-use patterns has been explored earlier. (Firey, 1947.) Yet, whereas in the North End of Boston close relations with neighbors was one manifestation of the Italian value system, in the case of the Mattapan Jews it seems that the neighborhood came to symbolize a common identity without the people having close relations with one another. How an area acquires such a symbolic meaning and how this symbol is preserved is beyond the scope of our data. Yet this might be a fruitful direction to pursue in the future study of neighborhoods.

Can a Neighborhood Become Successfully Integrated?

In concluding this study, the inevitable question which arises is: could the situation we have discussed been avoided? In other words, could Mattapan have become a stable integrated neighborhood? According to previous studies, the process of racial change seems to be irreversible; once black people begin moving into an all-white neighborhood, the area usually changes from white to black. (Duncan and Duncan, 1957; Molotch, 1972; Rapkin and Grigsby, 1960; Taueber and Taueber, 1965; Wolf and Lebeaux, 1969; Mayer, 1960.) These studies blame mainly structural-ecological factors, such as the restrictions of housing choices for blacks, for this process of racial residential transition.

In many respects Mattapan was similar to other changing neighborhoods. Yet, in contrast to other areas, Mattapan had a relatively high percentage of fairly new housing units built in the 1950's and 1960's. The area was no doubt still attractive to white people in the late sixties, since more than a quarter of the white population moved into its present homes between 1968 and 1970 when the neighborhood had already begun to change. This was also true for the people interviewed. That the area is still attractive to quite a number of Jews one can gather from the fact that they have remained in the neighborhood.

The advantages of staying in Mattapan are similar to those given by Rapkin and Grigsby (1960) as an explanation of why whites still buy houses in a mixed area. They are the commonplace reasons for housing choices, and many Jews moved into Mattapan for these same reasons. People liked the semisuburban area inside the city, the convenient location, the good transportation, and other services. The most important factor in people's decision to remain in the area is related to the good housing conditions. People could find good and not too expensive houses in Mattapan. Although upper middle-class Jews moved to the suburbs, the area still remained an attractive place of residence for the lower middle-class and working-class Jews. The people liked their homes and had no intention of moving out. Although their surroundings changed, and they felt the neighborhood was becoming an unlivable place, most people did not have immediate moving plans. Yet they know that since the area is constantly changing, in the end they will have to move out. The Mattapan Jews realize that they are becoming more and more a white minority, and they are afraid to remain, as many put it, "the last white person on the street."

It is impossible now to say, retrospectively, if this process of rapid racial transition could have been halted at an earlier stage. As we have seen, young people began moving out of the area before black families moved in, and quite a large proportion of the remaining population were elderly people. One cannot know whether without the BBURG program and the open enrollment in the schools this transition would not have occurred. People knew, of course, that only black families were eligible for the FHA mortgages in the area, and that these were denied, deliberately or not, to white people. Once the Jews realized that blacks were moving onto their streets, they feared more blacks were going to move in, so that at some point the whites would become a minority. The prediction that one would become the last white person on the street was based on the assumption that white people would not buy in the area. If the BBURG mortgages had been given to whites also, the fear of being outnumbered would not have been so great. After all, the Mattapan Jews realized the many advantages of their area and regarded it as a good place to live. It is difficult to know if by giving mortgages to whites the transition process could have been altered, but it seems at least that the change would not have come so fast. Encouraging whites to buy in the area could have had an important demonstrative effect on the Mattapan people.

The same could be said about the junior high school. The result of busing only black children to the Lewenberg school was that in a few years the school changed from white to black.

Perhaps because it was regarded as one of the better schools, it might have become integrated had a careful balance been kept. If white parents, like white home owners, do not object to the presence of blacks per se, but rather are afraid of being outnumbered, the opening of an area or a school to blacks only inevitably plays upon their fears of becoming a minority.

Could deliberate efforts to organize the people have prevented the flight of whites and thus the rapid change? We know that The Mattapan Organization failed in 1969, and that even a very aggressive neighborhood organization could not stop the process of racial change in the South Shore area of Chicago. (Molotch, 1972.) Yet, if people realize that "their" neighborhood is changing only when black people begin moving onto their streets, the usefulness of an overall neighborhood organization is questionable. The Mattapan Organization began its activities when only 5% of the population was black and long before people were aware of the fact that their area was changing. Since, as we have seen, the concept of a changing neighborhood as a broad territorial unit is not too meaningful, a small-scale organization on a street or block level might have had more impact in reducing the pace of racial transition.

NOTES

1 For detailed bibliography of these studies, see Gerald D. Suttles, The Social Construction of Communities, 1972.

2 For further discussion of this subject, see, for instance, Suzanne Keller, *The Urban Neighborhood: A Sociological Perspective*, 1968.

APPENDIX

General areas of questions asked during the interviews:

1. Residential history—previous places of residence, migration pattern, reasons for moving out of previous home.

2. Present housing conditions—reasons for choosing present house/apartment, length of residence, size and condition of present home, monthly rent or mortgage, owner-tenant relations.

3. Mattapan in the past—description of the Jewish neighborhood, its services, stores, and institutions.

4. The process of change in the neighborhood. Did the neighborhood change? How and when did it start? How did one realize the area was changing, and what were the major changes?

5. Why did the neighborhood change? Could this process have been avoided, and who is to blame for what had happened? Why did the Jewish people move out?

6. Did any changes occur in the Jews' own way of life? What kind of changes? When and why did they occur? To what extent were they related to changes in the neighborhood?

7. Crime and fear. Had the people interviewed been victimized and/or their homes broken into? Were there any crimes in the area or on the street? Do the people know anybody who has been victimized? Is there more crime in Mattapan than in other areas? Who commits the crimes and why? Do the people walk on the streets? How do they protect themselves (if they think protection is needed)? What safety devices do they have in their homes?

8. Social network—contact with present and past neighbors. When and how often do the people (or did they) get together? Did they have relatives and friends in the area? Did they move out? Where do most relatives and friends live now, and how often do they get together? Do they come to visit in Mattapan?

9. Shopping habits in the past and present and the use of the neighborhood facilities.

10. Relations with blacks. Do the people have black neighbors? Do they know them? Do they have any contact? The image of the black neighbors in comparison to black people in general. Do they mind having black neighbors? If so, why? How do they perceive the attitude of the black people toward Jews?

11. Plans for the future—intentions to stay or move. If moving, why and when and where? Reasons for staying in the area. How do the people perceive the future of the neighborhood?

12. Information background—place of birth, age, occupation, place of work, number of people in household. If there are children in the family, where do they go to school? Do they have friends in the area?

BIBLIOGRAPHY

Aaron, Henry J. *Shelter and Subsidies*. Washington, D.C.: The Brookings Institution, 1972.

Allport, Gordon W. *The Nature of Prejudice*. Garden City, N.Y.: Doubleday Anchor Books, 1958.

Armor, David J. "The Evidence on Busing." *The Public Interest*, No. 28 (Summer 1972), 90–126.

Axelrod, Morris; Fowler, Floyd J.; and Gurin, Arnold. *A Community Survey for Long Range Planning: A Study of the Jewish Population of Greater Boston*. Boston: The Combined Jewish Philanthropies, 1967.

Binzen, Peter. *Whitetown U.S.A.* New York: Random House, 1970.

Bradburn, Norman M.; Sudman, Seymour; and Gockel, Galen L. *Side by Side: Integrated Neighborhoods in America*. Chicago: Quadrangle Books, 1971.

Bratt, Rachel G. *Home Ownership Survey: A Report on the Boston Banks Urban Renewal Group*. Boston: Model Cities Administration, 1972.

Bressler, Marvin. "The Myer's Case: An Instance of Successful Racial Invasion." *Social Problems*, VIII, No. 2 (Fall 1960), 126-141.

Burgess, Ernest W. "Residential Segregation in American Cities." *Annals of the American Academy of Political and Social Sciences*. CXL (November 1928), 105-115.

Coleman, Richard P., and Neugarten, Bernice L. *Social Status in the City*. San Francisco: Jossey-Bass, 1971.

Coles, Robert. *The Middle Americans*. Boston: Little, Brown, 1970.

Deutch, Morton, and Collins, Mary E. *Interracial Housing: A Psychological Study of a Social Experiment*. Minneapolis: University of Minnesota Press, 1951.

Drake, St. Clair, and Cayton, Horace R. *Black Metropolis*. 2nd Ed. New York: Harper and Row, 1962.

Duncan, Otis D., and Duncan, Beverly. *The Negro Population in Chicago: A Study of Residential Succession*. Chicago: University of Chicago Press, 1957.

Edwards, Ossie. "Family Composition as a Variable in Residential Succession." *American Journal of Sociology*, LXXVII, No. 4 (January 1972), 731-741.

Firey, Walter. *Land Use in Central Boston*. Cambridge, Mass.: Harvard University Press, 1947.

Fishman, Joshua A. "Some Social and Psychological Determinants of Intergroup Relations in Changing Neighborhoods." *Social Forces*, XL, No. 1 (October 1961), 42-51.

Fried, Mark. "Grieving for a Lost Home." *The Urban Condition*. Edited by Leonard Duhl. New York: Basic Books, 1963.

———, and Levin, Joan. "Some Social Functions of the Urban Slum." *Urban Planning and Social Policy*. Edited by Bernard J. Frieden and Robert Morris. New York: Basic Books, 1968, 60-83.

Gans, Herbert J. *The Urban Villagers*. New York: The Free Press, 1962.

———. *The Levittowners*. New York: Vintage, 1967.

———. *People and Plans: Essays on Urban Problems and Solutions*. New York: Basic Books, 1968.

Geer, Blanche. "First Days in the Field." *Sociologists at Work*. Edited by Phillip E. Hammond. Garden City, N.Y.: Doubleday Anchor Books, 1967, 372-398.

Glazer, Nathan. "Social Characteristics of American Jews." *The Jews*,

Their History, Culture and Religion. Edited by Louis Finkelstein. 3rd ed. New York: Harper, 1960, 1694-1735.

————, and McEntire, David. *Studies in Housing and Minority Groups*. Berkeley: University of California Press, 1960.

————, and Moynihan, Daniel P. *Beyond the Melting Pot*. 2nd ed. Cambridge, Mass,: Massachusetts Institute of Technology Press, 1970.

Goffman, Erving. *Behavior in Public Places*. New York: The Free Press, 1963.

————. *Relations in Public*. New York: Basic Books, 1971.

Goldstein, Sidney. "American Jewry, 1970: A Demographic Profile." *American Jewish Year Book*, Vol. 72, 1971, 3-87.

————, and Goldscheider, Calvin. *Jewish Americans: Three Generations in an American Community*. Englewood Cliffs, N.J.: Prentice Hall, 1968.

Grodzins, Morton. *The Metropolitan Area as a Racial Problem*. Pittsburgh: University of Pittsburgh Press, 1958.

Guest, Avery M., and Zuiches, James J. "Another Look at Residential Turnover in Urban Neighborhoods." *American Journal of Sociology*, XXXIV, No. 6 (November 1971), 457-467.

Harris, Louis, and Swanson, Bert. *Blacks and Jews in New York City*. New York: Praeger, 1970.

Hoyt, Homer. *The Structure and Growth of Residential Neighborhoods in American Cities*. Washington, D.C.: U.S. Government Printing Office, 1939.

Johnston, R. J. *Urban Residential Pattern, An Introductory Review*. New York: Praeger, 1972.

Keller, Suzanne. *The Urban Neighborhood: A Sociological Perspective*. New York: Random House, 1968.

Krohn, Roger G., and Tilly, Ralph. "Landlord-Tenant Relationship in a Declining Montreal Neighborhood." *The Sociological Review Monograph*, No. 14 (September 1969), 5-31.

Lansing, John B.; Clifton, Charles C.; and Morgan, James N. *New Homes and Poor People: A Study of Chains of Moves*. Ann Arbor, Michigan: Institute for Social Research, 1969.

Laurenti, Luigi. *Property Values and Race: Studies in Seven Cities*. Berkeley: University of California Press, 1960.

Lejeune, Robert, and Alex, Nicholas. "On Being Mugged: The Event and Its Aftermath." *Urban Life and Culture*, II, No. 3 (October 1973), 259–287.

Lemert, Edwin M. *Human Deviance, Social Problems and Social Control*. Englewood Cliffs, N.J.: Prentice Hall, 1967, Chapter 3.

Levine, Naomi, and Hochbaum, Martin. *Poor Jews: An American Awakening*. New Brunswick, New Jersey: Transaction Books, 1974.

Lieberson, Stanley. *Ethnic Patterns in American Cities*. New York: The Free Press, 1963.

Marx, Gary T. *Protest and Prejudice*. Rev. ed. New York: Harper and Row, 1969.

Mayer, Albert J. "Russel Woods: Change Without Conflict—A Case Study of Neighborhood Racial Transition in Detroit." *Studies in Housing and Minority Groups*. Nathan Glazer and David McEntire, Eds. Berkeley: University of California Press, 1960, 298–320.

Meadow, Kathryn P. "Negro–White Differences Among Newcomers to a Transitional Urban Area." *Journal of Intergroup Relations*, III, No. 4 (Autumn 1962), 320–330.

Millen, James S. "Factors Affecting Mixing in Residential Areas." *Segregation in Residential Areas*. Edited by Amos H. Hawley and Vincent P. Rock. Washington, D.C.: National Academy of Sciences, 1973, 148–171.

Molotch, Harvey L. "Racial Change in a Stable Community." *American Journal of Sociology*, LXXV, No. 2 (September 1969a), 226–231.

———. "Racial Integration in a Transitional Community." *American Sociological Review*, XXXIV, No. 6 (December 1969b), 878–893.

———. *Managed Integration: Dilemmas of Doing Good in the City*. Berkeley: University of California Press, 1972.

Pettigrew, Thomas F. "Racially Separate or Together." *Journal of Social Issues*, XXV, No. 1 (January 1969), 43–69.

———. "Attitudes on Race and Housing: A Social-Psychological View." *Segregation in Residential Areas*. Edited by Amos H. Hawley and Vincent P. Rock. Washington, D.C.: National Academy of Sciences, 1973, 21–84.

Rapkin, Chester, and Grigsby, William G. *The Demand for Housing in Racially Mixed Areas*. Berkeley: University of California Press, 1960.

Rainwater, Lee. "Fear and the House-as-Haven in the Lower Class." *Journal of the American Institute of Planners*, XXXII, No. 1 (January 1966), 23–31.

Rossi, Peter. *Why Families Move*. New York: The Free Press, 1955.

Schelling, Thomas C. "A Process of Residential Segregation: Neighborhood Tipping." *Racial Discrimination in Economic Life*. Edited by Anthony H. Pascal. Lexington, Mass.: Lexington Books, 1972.

Sklare, Marshal. *American Jews*. New York: Random House, 1971.

Social Science Panel of the Advisory Committee to Housing and Urban Development. *Freedom of Choice in Housing: Opportunities and Constraints*. Washington, D.C.: National Academy of Sciences, 1971.

Stinchcombe, Arthur L.; McDill, Mary; and Walker, Dally. "Is There a Racial Tipping Point in Changing Schools?" *Journal of Social Issues*, XXV, No. 1 (January 1969), 127–136.

Strauss, Anselm. *Images of the American City*. New York: The Free Press, 1961.

Suttles, Gerald D. *The Social Order of the Slum: Ethnicity and Territory in the Inner City*. Chicago: University of Chicago Press, 1968.

————. *The Social Construction of Communities*. Chicago: University of Chicago Press, 1972.

Taueber, Karl E., and Taueber, Alma F. *Negroes in Cities: Residential Segregation and Neighborhood Change*. Chicago: Aldine, 1965.

U.S. President's Commission on Law Enforcement and the Administration of Justice. *The Challenge of Crime in a Free Society*. Washington, D.C.: U.S. Government Printing Office, 1967.

Vernon, Raymond. *The Myth and Reality of Our Urban Problems*. Cambridge, Mass.: Joint Center for Urban Studies, 1962.

Warner, Lloyd W. *Social Class in America*. New York: Harper and Row, 1949.

Wirth, Louis. *The Ghetto*. Chicago: University of Chicago Press, 1928.

————. "Urbanism as a Way of Life." *American Journal of Sociology*, XLIV, No. 1 (July 1938), 3–24.

Whyte, William F. *Street Corner Society*. 2nd ed. Chicago: University of Chicago Press, 1955.

Wolf, Eleanor P. "The Invasion-Succession Sequence as a Self Prophecy." *Journal of Social Issues*, XIII, No. 4 (October 1957), 7–20.

————. "Racial Transition in a Middle Class Area." *Journal of Intergroup Relations*, I, No. 3 (Summer 1960), 75-81.

————. "The Tipping Point in Racially Changing Neighborhoods." *Journal of the American Institute of Planners*, XXIX, No. 3 (August 1963), 217-222.

————, and Lebeaux, Charles. *Change and Renewal in an Urban Community*. New York: Praeger, 1969.

Young, Michael, and Willmott, Peter. *Family and Kinship in East London*. London: Routledge and Kegan Paul, 1957.

Zeul, Carolyn R., and Humphrey, Craig R. "The Integration of Black Residents in Suburban Neighborhoods." *Social Problems*, XVIII, No. 4 (Spring 1971), 462-474.

Zorbaugh, Harvey W. *The Gold Coast and the Slum*. Chicago: University of Chicago Press, 1929.

Index